CONVERSATIONS WITH A POCKET GOPHER
And Other Outspoken Neighbors

Conversations With
A Pocket Gopher

And Other Outspoken Neighbors

JACK SCHAEFER

CAPRA PRESS
SANTA BARBARA

Grateful acknowledgement to
Audubon Magazine where these
Conservations first appeared.

Illustrations by Irene Brady.
Cover design by Deja Hsu.

Library of Congress Cataloging-in-Publication Data

Schaefer, Jack, 1907-1990.
Conservations with a pocket gopher, and other outspoken neighbors
/ Jack Schaefer : illustrated by Irene Brady.
p.   cm.
Previous published by: Capra Press, 1978.
ISBN 0-88496-348-9
1. Imaginary conversations. 2. Animals--Fiction. I. Title.
PS3537.C223C66 1992
813'.54--dc20   91-38797
                                                           CIP

CAPRA PRESS
Post Office Box 2068 / Santa Barbara, CA 93120

CONTENTS

Foreword

Ever since I learned how to converse with animals other than humans—more accurately, to have them converse with me—I have been dismayed to discover that most of the people I meet insist it is nothing more than a trick on my part, a hoax, a pretending, a mere imaginary juggling of ideas. It is not of course. Very definitely not. Their attitude is understandable, I suppose, in that it is difficult enough nowadays for humans truly to communicate with each other without their trying to do so with members of other species. Yet the effort is well worthwhile. And the trick—if trick it be—is really very simple, requiring little more than sincere goodwill towards our companion creatures on this earth and a shift in perspective towards them.

Thomomys umbrinis, the Southern Pocket Gopher, taught it to me. He did this simply by being himself, by behaving in typical tantalizing gopher manner; that is, by staying underground and refusing to let me see him.

At the time I was bumblingly trying to become an amateur zoologist and actively seeking the acquaintance of my non-human neighbors. *Thomomys* was one of them; from evidence of his mounds a close neighbor with a fondness for doing his underground foraging almost, so to say, under my afternoon gardening feet. If he had been willing to come up into view, I undoubtedly would have made like a scientist doing field-work, been too busy watching him and making notes of his appearance and actions to be open and receptive to other possible messages and meanings, As it was, all I could do as far as he was concerned was to sit quietly on an old stump, contemplate his most recent mounds, and think about gophers in general and him in particular.

Thinking is sometimes better than seeing.

There we were: myself aboveground, aware of him somewhere near, thinking about him and his kind; he underground, undoubtedly aware of me from earth tremors of by recent footsteps. Doing what? Could he be doing in his way what I was doing in mine? Could he be thinking about me and my kind? If so, what would he be thinking of us humans in general and me in particular?

I sat on my stump drowsing in warm sunlight, lazily letting what I knew about gophers drift through my mind, gradually becoming more certain that he *was* down ther and he *was* thinking over what he knew about us humans.

If I were a pocket gopher, what would I think of us and of me? He could tell me. . . if only he would. He could tell me. . . . if only he knew I would listen. . . and try to understand. . . .

"Loafing again," said the Pocket Gopher.

* * *

All over the world other other animals are trying to talk to us. Their tragedy—and ours—is that so few of us even try to learn how to listen to them.

JACK SCHAEFER
Santa Barbara

Conversations
with a Pocket Gopher

(Thomomys umbrinis)

L OAFING AGAIN," says the Pocket Gopher. "You are woe-
fully lacking in willpower. Your work times are brief.
Your loafing times are long."

Reproof is vain in his voice, that gruff grumble-burred
scritching in his throat that somehow shapes itself into
words. Irritable by nature, he is trying to irritate me.
Afflicted with a work ethic, he has no appreciation of quiet
repose. A lifelong underground miner, he would undermine my enjoyment of drowsy rest. No matter. I am ar-
mored against him by curiosity about him.

Two weeks ago he took up residence just outside the
southwest corner of the field behind my house where

tossed-over pruning branches and tumbled brush along the side of an irrigation ditch provide some aboveground protection for his underground homesite. During the last few days he has occasionally tunneled under the fence into the corner of my field. Not once have I seen him, but I have been aware of his presence, evidence offered by multiplying mounds, disposal dumps for his hidden engineering, which mark his fossorial foraging.

"Pathetic performance. Loafing again," comes the crusty echo from somewhere under the brush pile. Obviously he has reopened one of his plugged tunnel entrances there to spy on me and my activity or lack of it.

"I am not loafing," I say. "I am thinking. I am thinking long thoughts about men and beasts."

"Impossible," says the Pocket Gopher. "You only think you are thinking. Only the reptiles require lazing warmth to summon their mental powers. We mammals—I admit you are a fellow mammal—operate quite otherwise. Two conditions govern our ability to think thinkingly. One is to be in the cool cuddle of the underground earth. The other is to be working. When the muscles, the claws, the teeth, the whole of the physical structure is active, then the mind is active too."

"So YOU say," I say.

"So I know," he says. "So I know without expecting you to understand. But of what have you been thinking you are thinking?"

"I have been thinking about your pockets."

"Ahhhhhhh," he says.

"Yes. Your pockets. Those fur-lined pockets with external openings. Shaped, I believe, like the pockets in my pants. It strikes me as very curious that of all the mammals in this wide wearying old world only you and your cousins the pocket mice and kangaroo rats, who are not mice and rats at all, should have those convenient receptacles."

"True," he says. "We pocketed people are an exclusive superfamily with just two families."

"And it strikes me as even more curious, in view of that first curious fact, that whenever in my reading of zoological books I come on accounts of you, these simply state that you have those pockets and mention little or nothing more about them."

"Of course," he says. "Typical human behavior."

He has stopped me there. Could I creep down into the cool cuddle of the earth and engage in muscle-claw-teeth activity, I might unravel his reasoning. No need. He is eager to instruct me.

"Jealousy is behind that neglect," says the Pocket Gopher. "You humans envy us our pockets. You must make your pockets out of alien materials and fasten them about you in cumbersome fashion. Our pockets are part of our natural endowment. More to the point, you actually pride yourselves on your artificial pocketry. Your anthropologists claim the invention of containers, of carrying receptacles, as an important technological advance in human development. When did you manage to make that advance? One, one and a half, by most generous possible estimate, two million years ago. We gophers have had our pockets thirty million years or more. I grant you our first ones were not as perfect and capacious as our present models, but way back then we had already caught the concept, made the idea manifest, pointed natural pocketry into the future. Envious of our priority in invention, our grasp of the pocket principle when your ancestors were still just learning to grasp tree branches, your zoologists virtually ignore our pockets, slide swiftly over them, hurry on . . ."

"Hold it," I say. "Let me make a point. Not in defense of human zoologists, who have been so wrong so often so long on so many things. I give you priority in pocketry. But you claim too much credit. Other creatures of respectable antiquity have developed carrying containers. For example, the marsupials. They . . ."

"Have belly pouches," he says. "Also with external openings, yes. But those are not true pockets, used for true pocket purposes. Their pouches are substitute wombs, coverings for the nipple region. Pockets? Pah!"

"Well, then," I say. "How about others in your own multitudinous order, the rodents. For example, the squirrels and the chipmunks. They . . ."

"Have cheek pouches," he says. "With no external openings. Such serve their—the pun is irresistible—their nutty purposes, the carrying of acorns and hard berries. Rather messy, poking food into one's mouth not for eating but for carrying, yet effective in a crude sort of way. Adequate for squirrels and chipmunks, who are really rather frivolous folk, frolicking about in silly sunshine not only aboveground but even up in trees, willing to accept the nobility of hard work only when winter approaches. We gophers would never be content with mere cheek pouches. We have the wisdom to spend almost our entire lives working, doing so the year around. Cheek pouches would hamper us in that noble pursuit."

"Pouches . . . pockets," I say. "The distinction in regard to work escapes me."

"Of course," he says. "How could you know? You have neither pouches nor pockets, not the built-in variety. And your teeth—well, those are not even worth a mention."

"My teeth serve my purposes," I say. "What have teeth to do with pockets?"

"The connection is clear," says the Pocket Gopher. "As even you should know, we gophers do most of our foraging underground, tunneling hither and thither and yon. The superb claws of our forefeet suffice for ordinary tunneling in ordinarily soft or loose soil. But often there are patches of hard-packed ground. Into use come our even more superb teeth, our splendid incisors. Often again there are obstacles such as tree roots, even wires and cables and such which you humans have the effrontery to put underground. With our magnificent incisors we simply gnaw through them. Wonderful tools, our incisors. The equivalent of your spades and hatchets and axes and drills. No sharpening ever needed. Layers of hard enamel on the front wear away more slowly than the rest of them, keeping a sharp slant edge as your carpenters do with their chisels. Evergrowing, too, so that growth keeps pace with the wearing-down. Wonderful tools. Always in place. Always ready. What a feeling of security their possession gives. What a sense of power to be chomping through something that is trying to block the way forward. What a . . ."

"Pockets," I say.

He pauses. He sighs. "Oh, yes. Pockets. Picture me tunneling busily ahead, finding food along the way, cutting this into pieces and putting them into my valuable pockets. Such items as tasty tubers, bountiful bulbs, succulent weed roots, even whole plants of delicate varieties which I pull down through the ground into my tunnel. No need to take time from work to make trips to my storerooms except when my capably capacious pockets are full. But suppose I merely had cheek pouches, was compelled to stuff the food into my mouth and carry it that way. A fine business when I need my jaws in good working order, my splendid teeth for tunneling. My pockets, independent of my mouth, are the perfect solution."

"All right," I say. "I am thinking that I think I follow you. And I know that the popular notion is all wrong that you carry out the dirt from your digging in your . . ."

"Horrible thought! Dirt in my pockets? Why do you think I have those special muscles to close them? Precisely to prevent dirt from getting in."

"Ingenious of you," I say. "But I was trying to get around to saying that using your teeth for tunneling must be a messy business. Always getting mouthfuls of that same dirt."

I could swear that he almost chuckles. "You certainly would if you tried it," he says. "You humans have silly teeth. And it must be your facial arrangement that gives you all such an ugly appearance. Flat-faced as if someone has pushed it in. Nose sticking out like some putty pasted on. Such a nose would certainly get in the way of good digging. Lips that actually cover your teeth, hide them when your mouth is closed. No doubt if I had such pathetic examples, I would hide them too. Mine, my incisors, are so superbly different it would be a shame to hide them. I never do. My lips fold in behind them. Result: I can work away, chomping with those magnificent tools, and not a smitch of dirt gets into my mouth."

He seems to be waiting for my response. "Pockets and

teeth," I say. "Logically connected and remarkable both; including the necessary facial arrangement. But there is a problem which bothers me. Based on two items I know. One, that you clear out the dug dirt from your tunnels by turning up the long claws of your forefeet and making like a road scraper or bulldozer to push the dirt along and up a disposal tunnel and out. I know that because I once saw one of you popping it out to form one of your mounds. The other is that your tunnels must just about match your body girth in diameter, be rather a tight fit as you move along. I know that because I . . ."

"Because you were mean enough to muck up one of my laterals leading to that mound closest to the fence corner."

"Well, yes. I dug down and measured it. Cylindrical in shape and almost exactly two and seven-eighths inches in diameter. Surely that does not give you much elbow-room."

"Elbowroom? I have no elbows, not your kind that stick out at angles when you use your arms. And I like tight fits. Tunnels just exactly my size."

"There it is," I say. "What bothers me. You are digging ahead in one direction. Probably kicking the loosened dirt back under behind you. How in that narrow space do you turn around to push it out?"

I wait. There is silence for nearly a full minute. Then I hear him, faint and seeming puzzled: "How DO I do it? I have never thought of that. I just do it. Facing one way, then facing the other way. I just do it. I must . . . No, I guess I . . . But then . . . I'll have to . . ." His voice fades away completely. He is off somewhere in his underground maze.

Another day. Late afternoon sunlight of springtime is promising later summer heat. My arms and shoulders ache a bit from work in my vegetable garden with my artificial incisor, a spade. It is a good tool. I have used a file to give it a proper slanted cutting edge. Now I am sitting on the rickety low bench in the southwest corner of the field behind my house. Drowsiness soaks into me.

"Loafing again," says the Pocket Gopher. "This time you have my approval. Two reasons. One, I know that you have been working hard because I have sensed the earth tremors coming from the arena of your exertions. The other, I have something to tell you."

"You should have," I say. "You have not yet answered my last question of yesterday. So I have been sitting here thinking I am thinking that you must have had to go down into the cool cuddle of the earth and become very active to do some of your kind of thinkingly thinking."

"Stop trying to be clever," he says. "Trying to turn my own fine phrases back upon me. This is too important a matter for mere cleverness. I have made an amazing discovery. We gophers are even more remarkable than I had imagined. We are acrobats of the highest order. Magicians at maneuvering. Somersault stylists. Conquerors of confining space. Geniuses at . . ."

"My question," I say.

He pauses. He sighs. "Yes, your question. You asked how I turn around in the narrowness of my tunnels which are almost exactly of the same diameter that I am. I could not answer. My turnabout was such an instinctive procedure that I had never bothered to think about it. I simply did it. So I had to go down into one of my nicely narrowest tunnels and do it to see how I did it."

Silence. I suspect he is reluctant to go on. "What happened?" I say.

He sighs again. "I became very angry with you. With you and your damnable question. Because I could not do it. Thinking about doing it tangled my mental processes, interfered with the instinctive patterns in my muscles. I became stuck only partway around."

Silence again. "Obviously you became unstuck," I say.

"Of course. I was in an extremely awkward position. But I had my incisors. I managed to loosen enough dirt to free myself."

"And then?"

"Ahhhhh. Then I did the sensible thing. I thought not of how I did my turnabout but of how I could learn how I did my turnabout. I understood I must erase from my mind the seeming logical impossibility of doing it. I must separate the procedure into small stages and study these in sequence."

"That turned the trick?"

"That taught me the trick. In another part of that nicely narrow tunnel I blanked my mind and started a turnabout—and stopped—and studied what I had done up to that point. Then I started again and went somewhat further—and stopped—and studied again. Five such stages and I had it. Oh, the wonder of it! The glory of it! The thrilling splendor . . ."

"Of precisely what?"

"Of doing the seemingly impossible. Of feeling one's whole being coordinating in a magical maneuver. It is not done in stages, of course. It is one single flowing motion of all of me. My head goes down and under between my forelegs and my body stretches, reducing the girth the small margin that is just enough, and my weight swings forward pivoting on one side of my head and that side's shoulder and my hindquarters slide over and as all this happens I am twisting and lo! there I am, rightside up and facing in the other direction. It is remotely somewhat like what you call turning a cartwheel but with no awkward outstretching and waving of limbs, and it is infinitely more smooth and fluid and graceful. Were I given to laughing, I could do so at the thought of anyone constructed like you trying to do it. To think I was doing it hundreds of times around the clock unaware of the wonder of the achievement. It is a feat truly worthy of us gophers. Being aware of it adds a new dimension to the pleasure of working. It adds to the uniqueness of . . .''

"Enough," I say. "You have exhausted that particular subject. I have another question."

He sounds, for him, almost jovial. "Question away," he says.

"Well, then. Last night I read another zoological account of you. It merely mentioned your pockets, but it said quite a bit about your teeth, your incisors."

"I have already told you about them."

"Ah, but this writer told me more. He told me that of all the rodents, all of whom have ever-growing incisors, you hold the growing record. He made the astounding assertion that your lower incisors can grow as much as nine inches in a year, your upper a full fourteen inches."

"His assertion," says the Pocket Gopher, "is reasonably true. A trifle exaggerated, perhaps, except in exceptional cases, but reasonably true. Is your question answered?"

"I have not yet asked it," I say. "Listen carefully. You

really hold two records. One in the growing of teeth, the other in the amount of work you do. Which of the two came first—or, rather, which is the cause of the other? Did you develop those record-growing teeth to match the prodigious amount of work you insist upon doing? Or did you develop the prodigious work habit to keep those otherwise runaway teeth under control?"

I can fairly feel the silence under the brush pile. Then comes a low mumble-grumble: "That human has done it again. Something else I have never thought about. I need to go below and so some thinkingly thinking."

Waning afternoon sunlight slants on me from low on the western horizon. I am relaxed in satisfying drowsiness. Then a chill of coming evening whispers past me as I hear a faint rustling under the brush pile.

"You arc a fool," says the Pocket Gopher. "If I thought you were truly intelligent, I would suspect that you seek by indirection to attack my philosophy which rests on a foundation of belief in the necessity and the nobility of work. Upon reflection I conclude that you, like all humans, are basically ridiculous, overproud of the rationalizing frontal lobes of your overgrown brain. The question you propound is simply another version of the ancient conundrum: which came first, the chicken or the egg? The answer, of course, is that neither came first except in the evolutionary sense that the shelled egg was developed by the reptiles long before there was a chicken. But the chicken egg and the chicken evolved together in their own endless circular cycle. The egg is the chicken's way of producing another chicken and the chicken is the egg's way of producing another egg. Neither came first, and each is the cause of the other. Just so with my teeth and my work habit. Are you answered?"

"Not exactly," I say. "It seems to me that you have just slipped sideways around the . . ."

"Fool," says the Pocket Gopher. "Bound up in your human obsession with whys and wherefores, with causes and effects. I could ask you a question. If one or the other did come first, what would that matter? In this here and now I have them both, my teeth and my work habit, and they complement each other and give meaning to my life, and the work which they jointly impel me to do has its own meaning in the ecological balance of all life in this world. And so I could ask you a question about your question. What does it matter? I do not ask it because I am not interested in an answer."

"But I have an answer," I say. "I have one. I have . . ." My own voice fades away. He has retired into his underground maze.

Another day. Rain has been falling through much of the morning and into the afternoon. Now at shadow-lengthening time the sun is peering between retreating clouds. I wander about noting what is new in the neighborhood. Item: a first pair of rabbits, fat and furry and white, in the hutch my neighbor to the southeast has been building near his back line. Item: some more patchwork carpentry has been done to add a lean-to shelter to the near side of the barn belonging to the neighbor to the south. There are some fresh bales under its wobbly roof. Item: the cribber among the horses in the corral to the east has been at it again. There are fresh splinterings along a top rail. Item: more mounds have appeared in the southwest corner of my field behind my house.

I sit on the old bench and count. There were five mounds yesterday. There are nine today. I ponder the significance of this.

"Loafing again," says the Pocket Gopher. "With no excuse. You have not done a lick of work today."

"I have been inside," I say, "working my brain to put down on paper some of your recent remarks. It is impossible to be using my artificial incisor today. The ground is too moist. Too gummy. As an expert in ground-working you should know that."

"I do not know it," he says, "because it is not true. For inefficient you, perhaps. Not for me. That little shower merely soaked down about six inches. At ten to twelve and more inches down where I do most of my working the soil is still relatively dry. Yet even if it were soaked, I would be working. We gophers long ago developed our own special fur which refuses to let any dirt, however sticky, stick to it."

"But what happens," I say, "when we get a real gully washer? One that floods your tunnels. What then?"

"My tunnels," says the Pocket Gopher, "are never really flooded. I maintain a system of drains for just such a contingency. You forget that I am an engineer and thus an expert on drains. I am into my third year of quite constant work, and not once in that long time have my drains failed to function sufficiently to prevent my home quarters and storerooms and even a few foraging tunnels from being flooded."

My armor must be wearing thin. He is beginning to irritate me. The complacency of him. "So you say," I say. "But you can say anything about what goes on down there in your underground galleries and I have no way to check you out."

"Naturally not," he says. "You are another of the many unfortunate creatures limited to life aboveground. But let me labor—no pun—a point. You plead that you have not been working because the ground is too moist. I have been working it, even up where the rain has soaked it. Perhaps you have noticed some fresh mounds. I finished the one closest to you and plugged its tunnel exit less than half an hour ago."

"Yes," I say. "And three more made since yesterday. Four reasons plus five previous ones for what I shall now state. If you persist in foraging on this side of the fence, I shall either have you arrested for trespassing or demand that you pay me rent for use of my land."

Indignation makes him almost unintelligible. He positively splutters. "*Your* land?"

"My land," I say. "There is a deed duly executed and filed in the county courthouse which certifies this is my land."

"Incredible!" he splutters. "The conceit of it!" He is silent for perhaps twenty seconds, obviously tamping down his emotion because when he speaks again it is with a sort of resigned and patient forbearance.

"I see," says the Pocket Gopher, "that your mind, unlike my drains, has failed to function. Certainly at least on the subject of land titles. That deed you cite is valid only in regard to humans, who have perpetrated a diabolical conspiracy to parcel out all land according to their own greedy purposes. That deed means nothing to all other living creatures with the possible exception of your domesticated animals—and even they would pay scant attention to your so-called property lines if you did not fence them.

The robin who nested in that big cottonwood by the road last summer and may again this year. The skunk who checked your chickenhouse last night for a possible entrance. The cottontail who has been scouting this brush pile for a possible homesite. The young female meadow mouse who is already contemplating raising a family under that old stump. Do you actually believe that deed of yours means anything to them? Or, for that matter, to me? Your human legalities do not apply to other creatures, except insofar as you are able to enforce them by force."

"At which," I say, "we are very efficient."

"Oh, yes," he says. "You humans, lacking capable teeth and effective claws and real power and speed of muscle, are fiendishly clever at devising artificial weapons. But let me apply some of your own human logic to this subject of land titles. By your own laws you recognize priority of land occupancy and use as giving some right of ownership. Your courts have been awarding sums of money to Indian tribes in payment for land taken from them in the past by various means definitely including outright force. The reasoning now: they had prior occupancy and use. Of course this is merely salving your consciences. I note that you do so only after you have already taken the lands in question and reduced the former supposed owners to few in number and weak in power. But at least you have recognized the priority principle. I will wager that even you with your paradoxical puzzling mind have approved it."

"Well, yes," I say. "I think it only fair."

"Ahhhhhhh," he says. "Let us apply it to this piece of land described by your duly executed deed. How long have you yourself occupied and used it? Not much over two years. How long have your palefaced kind occupied and used it? Perhaps three hundred years. How long did the darker-skinned humans who built the pueblo on the rise of ground where your house now stands occupy and use it? Perhaps a thousand years. We gophers have occupied and used it for millions upon millions of years. Our claim has priority over that of you humans by many a thousandfold."

It is my turn to pause a moment. Then I say: "But many other creatures were also occupying and using it all during that time—and for ages even before you gophers."

"Of course," he says. "All of us using it in the natural nonhuman way. Each in his own ecological niche. All of us in our times living together, subject to no man-made laws but only to those of natural ecological balances. Consider right now. Do you think I think of that robin and that skunk and that cottontail and that young female mouse as trespassers or as tenants who should pay me rent? No. They are companion creatures sharing occupancy and use of the land with me."

"You certainly are proud of yourself," I say. "But you overlook   . . ."

"I overlook nothing," says the Pocket Gopher. "What do you know of this land you call yours? You see it solely as it is now. I see it in my racial memory as it has been through long ages. I can see it for one single small rather recent example as it was only ten thousand years ago, lusher and more tropical then, with camels and native horses and long-horned bison roaming this region. I can see in the time of my great grandfather, many times removed, in this very fence corner where you now sit, a mastodon lazily pulling down tree branches for a meal and on another occasion a sabertooth slaying a giant ground sloth and feeding heartily on it. What do you know of such things, you whose ancestral beginnings were far off across the oceans in other continents and whose more immediate ancestors have been here only a few centuries? Yet you claim title to this land."

"I do," I say. "And as you have admitted, I could be quite capable of enforcing my claim."

He sighs long and slowly. "I know that. So I urge you to consider certain alternatives. On the one hand you could make life miserable for me, perhaps eliminate me altogether. You humans are diabolically shrewd and persistent in such matters. You have devised more means, weapons and traps and poisons and deadly devices, for killing us gophers than you have for any other creatures. Oh, yes, with the paraphernalia you could contrive or buy, you could make life miserable for me. On the other hand, were I so minded, I could make life miserable for you. Drill holes in your irrigation ditch. Gnaw your hoses into pieces and render useless the tires of your car. Undermine your chickenhouse until it leans and cracks. Gobble your garden plants. Kill your fruit trees by cutting their roots. Tunnel under . . ."

"Stop," I say. "You are as diabolical as you accuse us humans of being."

"Not quite," says the Pocket Gopher. "Not as deadly. And I have not done any of those things. Not here. Not yet. I am merely presenting possibilities, assessing our respective capabilities in event of warfare. So what I propose is this: not a feud but a pact. A peace treaty. I have a fondness for this corner of what you regard as your field. It produces fine recurrent crops of weeds and forbs with nicely succulent roots. If you will refrain from trying to eliminate them as you did last year with that swinging sickle—another form of artificial incisor—and will let them flourish in the assurance I will keep them under control, then I will respect the rest of what you insist is your property."

I ponder this. He sounds sincere but his notions of the size of a fence corner could be elastic. "Just how much of my field," I say, "are you proposing that I allow to remain a weed garden?"

"Hmmmmm," he says. "As an engineer I am familiar with quick calculations." A vague mumbling comes from under the brush pile in which I can make out confusing mathematical phrases. "Ah, yes," he says. "This field is approximately one acre. From that aspiring young Chinese elm along the south line cutting across diagonally to the fourth post in the west fence line will do. Almost precisely one-twelfth of an acre. Quite adequate for me."

"Leaving eleven-twelfths of this field for me," I say. "Plus all the area around the house and outbuildings. That seems fair enough."

"Good," he says. "We are agreed. And now . . ."

"Wait," I say. "My paradoxical puzzling mind poses a new problem. Suppose other creatures refusing to honor my human title also insist upon similar treaties. If I give in to them too I may soon have treatied away all of my land."

"Your problem, not mine," he says. "But as usual you are forgetting pertinent items. One is that in any bargaining with them you have the surface and aboveground area of my corner as an asset. I will be using only the underground terrain. Another is that they are all accustomed to using land and its appurtenances such as grasses and bushes and trees in what I have called the natural nonhuman way. That is, joint occupancy subject to natural ecological balances. You can bargain away the same land, say this same corner, to quite a few of them."

His logic is unassailable. The prospect his reasoning offers has intriguing aspects. I am considering these when his voice, more grumble-burred than before, stops me.

"And now," says the Pocket Gopher, "I really must break this brief habit of wasting work time talking to you. I am behind my usual schedule. Spring is advancing, and I have only one storeroom full and part of another. In the last twenty-four hours I have dug only ninety feet of tunnel. In the previous twenty-four, delayed by my somersault experiments, I dug only eighty feet. My average this time of year is one hundred fifty. As you might say, I am now signing off on conversation. Perhaps next year . . ."

He is gone, down into his underground maze.

"Wait!" I call out to him. "Wait! I have questions, questions, questions! Why do you store more food than you ever can eat? Why do you lead such a solitary life? How do you find a mate when nature demands that? Why . . .? How . . .?"

There is only silence under the brush pile. He is a stubborn grouchy boastful old grumbler. I doubt that he will ever talk to me again. But at least I will see the multiplying evidence of his underground engineering, his mounds.

. . . and a Shrew

(Sorex vagrans)

"—TODAY . . . Poor hunting . . . have to hurry . . . Ha! over there . . . A cricket . . . Only a little one, mostly legs . . . Have to do better . . . Ha! that way . . . Hurrah! a locust larva . . . "

A hurrah for me too. I have been moving about in the southeast corner of the field behind my house where a half-dozen fair-sized trees annually add to the leaf mold around their bases. For at least half an hour I have been moving slowly, crouched down to bring my ears closer to the ground. I have been listening to and trying to follow thin high-pitched squeaking sounds which also are moving about, occasionally to the accompaniment of a slight rustling not so much in as under the latest layer of fallen leaves. I have had an increasingly tantalizing feeling that interspersed through the squeakings are words, phrases, perhaps short sentences, just barely beyond my ability to apprehend them.

Now at last I know I am right. Perhaps my ears have opened further. Perhaps an understanding has clicked into connection in my mind. Whatever or however, I hear him down there talking to himself. Will he talk to me?

I know what he is. Three times I have caught shadowy glimpses of him as he scurries from here to there. Something like some kind of a mouse, only smaller than any mouse, with a longer snout and a longer tail. A shrew.

"—better . . . Nice snack . . . Any more around? . . . Ho! What's this? . . . Blocking that hole . . . Open yesterday . . ."

He is very close to me, close by my right foot. I am not quite sure but think I can make out the tinyness of him under a fallen mulberry leaf, peering out and up at the vast looming immensity of my own bulk.

I try to keep my voice low in volume yet pitch it higher than usual. "It must be my foot," I say.

"Please move it," says the Shrew.

So. He *will* talk to me. I shift the offending foot and catch a glimpse of movement as he glides into a hole in the ground so small that otherwise I would not have noticed it. I remain motionless, wondering when and where he will reappear. A flicker of movement and he is out of the hole and back under the mulberry leaf.

"Thank you," he says. "A successful expedition. Three fat dung beetles and a millipede. I can rest a bit."

"Good," I say. "Because I am curious. I know what you

are but not who you are. Obviously of the long-tailed genus *Sorex* and very likely, of the five possible species here in New Mexico, the one known as *vagrans*. But by any chance are you of our unique state subspecies *neomexicanus?*"

"The *neos*," he says, "live somewhat farther south in the state. Right on *Sorex* and *vagrans*. Correct subspecies *obscurus*. Easily identified by my darkish coloring."

"Of course," I say. "But I really have not had a good look at you. At first I thought you might be not a *vagrans* but a *nanus*. A dwarf shrew."

"Oh, no," he says. "In general they live somewhat farther north. And I am larger than they are. I'm really quite big. Why, I weigh fully half an ounce."

"Impressive," I say. "At least I suppose in your scale of things that is impressive. Now in my scale—" I stop. He has interrupted me with a high thin squeak. "OHHHHH! What's that? Have they—?"

I have heard it too, a reverberating booming in the distance. "Nothing much," I say. "There's some blasting going on down in town where the urban renewal people are making wonderful messes."

"Thank heaven," he says. "It had me worried. And thank you. I appreciate your telling me. But now I'm hungry again. First tremors of starvation signals. In your scale I really am small, you know. Ratio between body weight and surface area very unfavorable. Constant heat loss. Have to eat more than my own weight every twenty-four hours to keep up adequate heat and energy."

"Wow," I say. "You had a good meal just a few moments ago. Yet you are hungry again. Is it that bad?"

"Not bad," says the Shrew. "Not bad. Not good. Just is.

I'm hungry most of the time. Simple case of necessity. Condition of living. Now if you will kindly remain still while I put some distance between us. Your feet are horrendous things. Either one could flatten me into instant oblivion."

He is off into his scurrying again. I remain motionless as his squeakings dwindle away in and under the leaf mold. As I listen I know what they are; his sonar system is at work. By echolocation in the dimness of his hunting grounds he can distinguish movements and shapes enough to aid his foraging. And interspersed with the squeakings he is talking to himself. I strain my hearing as the sounds fade. " . . . Ha! elm beetle larvae . . . Not much on taste . . . But a whole batch of them . . ."

Another day. I am moving about in the southeast corner of the field. I move cautiously, crouched low and listening intently, but I hear nothing except the crunching rustle of my own horrendous feet. I move on, approaching a rotting old stump by the south fenceline.

"Nice of you to be so careful," says the Shrew.

I stop, motionless, looking around. "Where are you? Why no sonar signals?"

"In this nice little hollow under this stump," he says. "Resting. Well fed at the moment. Surprised a pair of brush mice in here. Courting I think. Female skipped away fast. Male tried to make a fight of it. Too bad for him. But my gain."

"But—but—," I say. "He must have been twice your size."

"Not quite," he says. "But plenty plump. Still enough left of him for another good meal after a while."

"You confuse me," I say. "Down there on your scale you must be a prodigious fighter, a highly efficient killer. You have just killed a fellow creature nearly twice your size. You dash about killing all kinds of things, yet . . ."

"I don't think of it as killing," says the Shrew. "To me it's a matter of eating. As I told you, a matter of necessity. Condition of living. You do the same. You eat meat. It has to be killed first. Do you think of the killing when eating?"

"Well, no," I say. "I get your point. I let someone else do the killing and simply buy my meat at the store. You have to be your own butcher."

"Right," he says. "An honest way of doing it. Facing up to facts of life. No offense meant, but you—OHHHHH! What's that? Have they started . . .?"

I need a few seconds to focus on what has alarmed him. I have heard the sound often before and am used to tuning it out. He must be fairly new to the neighborhood. "That," I say, "is just some of the kids hereabouts playing with the plank bridge over the side irrigation ditch. It is hinged on one side so it can be lifted when the ditch is cleaned. The fool kids like to get it up and let it thump down."

"Thank you," he says. "I appreciate your explanation."

"Well, now," I say. "That is precisely what confuses me. Your thanking me. Here you are living under the necessity of almost constant hunting, constant killing, activity one would think might make you a rude inconsiderate murderous-minded creature. And you thank me. You say please to me. You impress me as a polite and friendly fellow."

"Why shouldn't I be?" says the Shrew. "You've been friendly to me. Moved your foot. Made no attempt to grab me. Even knew something about me. I can't eat you. You

don't want to eat me. No reason for anything but friendship between us. But pardon me a moment. My stomach
needs restocking. Mouse meat digests rather fast."

I wait, considering what he has said. Not long.

"There," he says. "Fueled again. Not often a chance like
this for leisurely conversation. What topic now?"

"I've been thinking," I say, "how different you are from
the reputation you have. You shrews are popularly
thought to be fierce, unfriendly, aggressive, bloodthirsty
little beasts."

"Oh, that," he says. "We shrews long ago accepted that
as another condition of living. Especially in regard to you
humans when you finally came along. Except, of course,
for rare ones like yourself. Your Aristotle had much to do
with it. A complete simpleton in some ways. Believed
without checking popular notions that we kill for enjoyment of it, of the killing not the eating, and that our sonar
signals are screams of joy in anticipation of killings. But in
general our bad reputation has been a good thing."

"How so?"

"I don't like to boast," says the Shrew. "But we are
rather cute cuddly furry little creatures. Personally, I
think more so than any mouse or hamster or gerbil. Without our reputation people would be wanting to make pets
of us. Catch us. Put us in cages. Incredibly dangerous
business."

"Again, how so?"

"Our food problem. We can starve to death in just a few
hours. One feeding forgotten and we're done for. Maybe
even before being put in a cage. Caught by someone and
popped in a box. Dead by the time he gets where he's going.
Oh, no. We like our reputation. The worse, the better."

"Even though it is wrong?"

"Certainly. And I just thought of something. You humans can be contradictory. Two of your words. Shrew-ish. Shrew-d. One derogatory. Other complimentary. Impossible really to understand you humans. Much too various. Only way to take you is one at a time, individually."

"Interesting," I say. "That is scarcely the way we take all you other creatures. We tend to lump you into categories."

"Of course," he says. "That's because you are lamentably ignorant about most of us. But we do some lumping ourselves. Based on knowledge, not ignorance. For example, we lump your scientists and your militarists and your politicians into one category labeled VERY DANGEROUS."

"Now, that," I say, "requires considerable . . ." I stop. He is not listening. He is speaking.

"Another time," he is saying. "Important business in paw. Your poor ears may be missing it, but there's another shrew hunting not far from here. In my territory. Could be a female with romantic notions. Early in the season for that but always a pleasant possibility. Or it could be a male. If so, I'll have to get rid of him."

"Kill him?" I say. "Or at least try to?"

"Good heavens, no!" he says. "What a disgusting thought. We shrews are not mutual murderers. We'll just square off and touch whiskers, assessing each other. Then we'll try to out-squeak each other. Squeaking offers an excellent test of innate vitality and determination. I have no doubt of the outcome. I am currently well fueled with food. And this is MY territory. In these matters right adds to might."

I catch a glimpse of him emerging from under the old stump. Then I am completely at a loss. He is so quick and erratic in movement, glides through and under ground litter so easily, that I have no notion where he has gone. I listen for squeaking sounds. Nothing. He and that other shrew are out of my low limited earshot or their exchanges, romantic or bellicose, are being conducted in squeaks up out of my low limited ear range.

Another day. I have pondered his statements of yesterday and come up with questions that tease my mind. Now I am in the southeast corner of the field equipped with my questions and a small saucer containing about half an ounce of hamburger. I move slowly about, careful where I place my feet. He is somewhere near, squeaking and talking to himself.

"... Lovely day ... Insects stirring ... Those newcomers, earthworms, wriggling ... All fine fare ..."

I crouch low, reaching out to place the saucer on the ground.

"Good afternoon," says the Shrew. "What are you doing?"

There he is, in plain view at last, not more than three feet away. He *is* a cute, cuddly, furry little fellow, momentarily almost motionless, sitting up on his tiny haunches, combing his whiskers with his forepaws.

"I am offering you food," I say. "Hamburger. Cow meat. Not your usual diet, of course, but ..."

"Meat's meat," he says. "Always welcome. We shrews can digest anything in the meat line. But please do not do this often. Could corrupt me. Encourage me to be lazy. Dependent on handouts. Very unshrewlike to be lazy.

Start to take life easy. Possibly fatal."

"It is not offered as a bribe," I say. "And I have no intention of trying to weaken your character. Just a friendly present of some food to fuel you for some leisurely conversation. I need information. I am still confused about you. By something you do and something you said."

He is already well into his hamburger meal, surprisingly dainty about it, taking quick small bites and chewing thoroughly. "Oh, yes," he says, voice somewhat muffled by meaty chewing. "No doubt I said too much. Sometimes do when my stomach's full. I suppose . . ." He stops. He sits up, small snouted head raised. "OHHHHH! What's that? Don't tell me they've . . ."

I have heard it too, the sudden surging sound and reverberating resonance in the air which has rattled the windows of my chickenhouse several hundred feet away. "Nothing much," I say. "Just a sonic boom. They aren't supposed to do it over this metropolitan area. But some of the pilots at the air base here think it fun to bust through the sound barrier."

"Thank . . . you . . . for . . . explaining . . . it," he says. "That really shook me. So real. So possible. I've actually lost my appetite. Well, had it slacken some. I'll just rest a bit."

"Good," I say. "On the resting I mean. What just happened is one of the things that puzzle me. Loud noises startle you."

"Booming noises," he says.

"All right," I say. "Booming noises. They seem to frighten you. Make you afraid of something. Of what?"

"Bombs," he says. "Atomic bombs."

"Ah . . . yes," I say slowly. "I am afraid of them too. No

one should be ashamed of being afraid of atomic bombs."

"Not afraid for myself," says the Shrew. He is his alert confident little self again. "We shrews know of fear only by hearsay. We are not afraid of anything, not even of that worst enemy, starvation. If we were, do you think we would have spread as we did long ago around most of the world into almost every condition and environment and climate however harsh, even into the Arctic Circle itself? I am not afraid. I am worried. We shrews carry a terrible burden of responsibility."

I stare down at him. "Good Lord," I say. "*That* certainly requires an explanation."

"Not an easy one," he says. "And it might offend you. But you've been friendly. I'll try. First I'll fortify myself with the rest of this hamburger."

I watch him eat, daintily yet swiftly. He finishes and proceeds to wash his small face with his forepaws and dry these on several blades of dry grass.

"I see the connection," I say, "between atomic bombs and your statement that you consider human scientists and militarists and politicians to be very dangerous. The scientists have made the bombs, the militarists have them in hand for possible use, and the politicians can give the signal for their use. But wherein lies your burden of responsibility?"

"Think back," says the Shrew. "Think back to the long ago time when the reptiles ruled the Earth. The dominant life-forms. Holding almost all available ecological possibilities on land and in the sea and in the air. Ranging from small ones up to the gigantic dinosaurs. In time we shrews were there too. The first of placental mammals. The first to achieve the mammalian mode. To achieve the combination of warmbloodedness and furry covering and nurturing of young by the placenta within the womb and birth of them alive and feeding of them through infancy from special glands called mammae. The marsupials made a start along that path, but we achieved the full goal. We only could do it, being small and inconspicuous and feeding on insects, offering no open competition to the dominant reptiles. I doubt they had any knowledge in their small sluggish brains that we even existed."

"I follow you," I say. "Just the other day I read that the fossil remains of the oldest known mammals, six small skulls dating from the Cretaceous period in Mongolia, are similar to the skulls of you shrews of today."

"Not just similar," he says. "The same. They were shrews. That long ago memory remains in our line."

"Shrews or only shrewlike," I say. "No real difference. Your point is made. Now, the next step in your reasoning."

"Logical and simple fact," says the Shrew. "In the long swing of geologic time the Age of Reptiles waned. The dominant forms became extinct. Tremendous possibilities opened up. We shrews launched the Age of Mammals. Some of us, hedging against the future, remained shrews. Others of us radiated out into ever-continuing experiments in new adaptations. They founded species after species, family after family, order after order, of placental mammals. New dominant life-forms on land and in the sea and with those redoubtable inventors, the bats, even in the air. Oh, it has been a wondrous parade for us shrews to watch through the multiplying millenia. New forms developing, old forms dwindling away, but always the mammals, our progeny, the life-forms we launched, inhabiting and inheriting the Earth. We have been prouder of some than of others, yet still some pride in them all. And new forms still possible on into the far future."

He pauses and his tiny form shivers with a long sigh. "Yes," he says. "For a long time we were proud of the line established by those of us early shrews who took to living in trees. The primate line. Your line."

"And still I follow you," I say. "And I am not offended. I am ashamed."

"Yes," says the Shrew. "We were the beginning. You humans are the current culmination. I am worried that you will be the end. Not just of yourselves but of all of us. Let your bombs loose and their radiation flooding the world and it is the end of us all. Even of us small inconspicuous shrews. Our hedge against the future will be canceled. We will not be here to try again. To start it all over again."

I stare down at this tiny furry philosopher and I can think of nothing to say.

"Yes," says the Shrew. "I am sorry for you humans. In the onrush of what you regard as your cleverness and wisdom and technological prowess, you know not what you do."

A flicker of movement and he is gone.

Another day. A morning. A beautiful clean morning. The smog that has been hanging over this part of the Rio Grande Valley has temporarily lifted. The sunlight is clear and bright and my mind is the same. I have good news for my tiny furry friend.

It is there in the lead story in the morning paper lying

now on the kitchen table beside my empty coffee cup. We humans are beginning to show glimmers of common sense. Progress is reported toward an arms limitation agreement with the Soviet Union. Emphasis on limitation of atomic weapons.

I hurry toward the southeast corner of the field behind the house. I stop at the edge of the area where a half-dozen fair-sized trees annually add to the leaf mold around their bases and have already started what will be this year's addition in the form of burgeoning new leaves. I listen intently. Yes. Faintly I make out thin high-pitched squaking sounds interspersed with words.

"... Fine day ... Never felt better ... Ha! that way ... A fat slug ... Hamburger's all right ... Better to earn your own ..."

Just where is he? Over there close by the corner? Eagerly I start forward, one step, two steps, three, four—and stop. A silence has enveloped me, a silence made more profound by the whisper of a wandering breeze through new leafy growth.

I raise my right foot and place it gently in a new position. I bend down and gently push aside crushed dead leaves where the foot has been. Held there, crouched, I stare down and there are tears in my eyes.

I am only a human. I know not what I do.

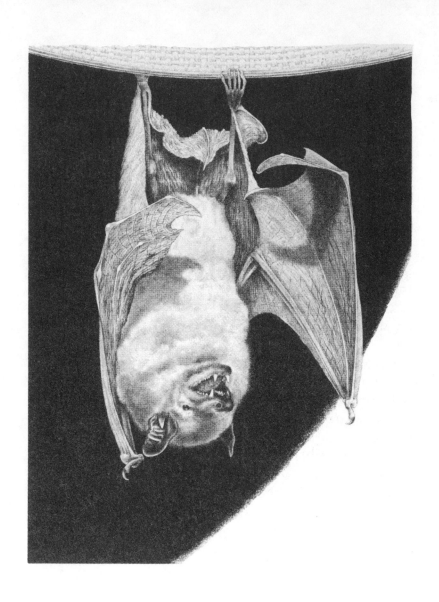

. . . and a Bat

(Eptesicus fuscus)

He cannot have been dead long. His body is still faintly warm—or perhaps that is only by contrast with the benumbed cold of my hand as I pick him up. I should have had the good sense to put on gloves before venturing out this morning.

I examine him closely. No broken bones; no visible wounds. Yet there is not the slightest twitch or tremor or suggestion of breath in him. He has the limp emptied look of the once living from whom life has recently departed.

Holding him in hand, I retreat into the house where piped fuel from a gas company and electricity from a power company have been obeying the order of a thermostat to create a congenial interior atmosphere. Flat on my desk I place a clean sheet of the white typewriter paper I keep in good supply. Gently I lay him down on this on his back. Against the whiteness of the paper the shape and coloration of him stand out sharp and distinct. I will test my limited zoological knowledge by seeing how well I can identify him without recourse to the books on my shelves.

A bat, of course. Furred and winged, he could not possibly be anything else. Therefore of the order Chiroptera, the hand-winged, second largest of all mammalian orders. Family? Almost certainly Vespertilionidae, usually and logically known as the simple-nosed or plainnose bats. Genus? His body is brown, his wing membranes black. He must be an *Eptesicus*, common name Big Brown Bat, and if so of the species *fuscus*, the only one of that genus inhabiting this country. Again if so, he must be of the subspecies *pallidus*, the only one inhabiting this part of the country.

This is my first closeup look at *E. fuscus pallidus.* A big brown bat. He is not big. A ruler out of a desk drawer tells me his body is only a smitch over four and a half inches long. How about the wingspan? I stretch out his hand-wings, noting that stiffness has not yet set in. Almost an exact thirteen inches. Quite a proportionate span, more than his body length out on each side of him. Even so he is not big. There are bigger bats in his own family. Only in one sense can he be said to be big. That is, he is somewhat bigger in body and more so in wingspan than is *Myotis lucifugus*, common name Little Brown Bat. Well, yes, I believe he is also slightly bigger than the other myotises and even the pipistrelles in the multitudinous Vespertilionidae family.

I am mildly proud of myself. I have identified him in

taxonomic terms.

The thermostat's order has been obeyed, and the room is nicely warm. I shed hat and jacket. I settle down in the comfortable rocking and swiveling desk chair my wife gave me some years ago and which I like to remember was listed as an executive's chair. Doing so, I note that his wings have tightened back to their original position close to his body. Strange? Or not strange? I am not familiar with the behavior of corpses.

Ah, that is the next problem. Can I figure out what must have happened to him?

I found him on the ground under one of the ancient cottonwoods along the irrigation ditch that skirts our property, tremendous trees nearly four feet in diameter at their bases and weathered through at least a century into fantastic massive-limbed shapes. All through their upper reaches, particularly wherever storms have snapped off branches, are holes and hollows and bark crannies, the kind of roosting sites big brown bats often use. *E. fuscus* must have bedded down—or rather up—in that tree last night. No, not last night. Sometime during the small hours early this morning. Being a bat, he would be active at night, and his sleeptime would be the daytime.

Now another factor for my figuring: the weather. According to the calendar on my desk spring will officially arrive tomorrow. During most of the past week the weather recognized that, was warmish and promising. Then last night it played one of its frequent quick-change tricks, came close to a record, dropped more than thirty degrees in a matter of hours.

But cold is not supposed to be a problem for big brown bats. Many of them, of the *pallidus* subspecies too, live far up in the mountains and far on north into Canada. They hibernate through the coldest months. Surely they can manage mere passing cold spells.

I rock back in my executive's chair, conscious of comfort and warmth. I swivel the chair a quarter-turn and look out the wide window that scans our back field. As usual when lazily thinking, I really see nothing out there. My mind is turned inward. As often in such circumstances and condition, I find myself talking softly to myself. "Of course," I am saying. "He is from much farther south in the state where it is lower and warmer. For some reason he has wandered up this way close to the mountains where the weather plays tricks, and not being accustomed to them he has been caught by too much cold and the temperature dropping too fast."

I am mildly proud again. I have solved that problem, or at least found an explanation that satisfies me. What remains now is to consider proper burial for him. Perhaps out in the back field near . . .

"Your pardon, sir. You are not quite right."

The words are faint yet clear. I have a fleeting impression that there to my left the desk itself has spoken. I swivel the quarter-turn back to face it. He is there exactly as before, flat on his back on the sheet of white paper, but his eyes are bright. Life is in them. He is looking at me.

I feel a flash of sudden and unreasonable and humble happiness. A fellow creature I thought dead is alive. And is speaking to me.

"Your pardon in turn," I say. "Could you explain how I am wrong?"

"Certainly, sir," says the Bat. His voice is still faint, and I lean closer to catch the words. "You are wrong geographically. I am no southerner. I come from father north in the mountains just over the Colorado line. Normally I hibernate until early next month. This year I emerged early. Overeager, I am afraid, to be on my way. I am working my way south."

"Migrating?" I say. "I didn't know . . ."

"No, sir," he says. "Not migrating. I had—I have my reasons. But foraging was so poor it has been hard to keep up strength. Perhaps last night when the cold set in I could have sunk into hibernation again. In that state I can take much colder temperatures. But I thought I could hold out and be on my way again come next dark. Obviously I was wrong. Which means you seem to be right with your too much, too fast, cold calculation."

"Thank you," I say. "Though you had to come close to death to make me right. The warmth of this room, I take it, has revived you. But why are you moving south.?"

"Please, sir," he says. "I do not want to talk about that. Not now. It is difficult to think of anything but food. I ate next to nothing last night."

"Good lord!" I say. "What a fool I am! A poor host! Of course you're weak and hungry."

My mind races, checking over the contents of re-frigerator and kitchen shelves. I can think of nothing in his food line and know of no insects or their relatives about and available to me this time of year. Then I remember something I have read. And I, sitting in an executive chair, should be an executive, leap into action, get things done.

"Lie right there," I say, crisp and efficient. "Relax and rest and soak up warmth. I'll forage for you."

I start to rise from the chair, but his voice stops me. "One moment, sir. I really cannot rest in this silly position. Most awkward. And uncomfortable. I lack the strength to flip myself over, and even so, then to fly and find a roosting spot. Would you be so kind as to help me?"

"Where?" I say, looking about, conscious of my ignorance of bat preferences in household perches.

"Anyplace will do for now," he says. "Someplace near. How about the edge, the lower one, of that lampshade?"

Gently I pick him up, holding him so that he is in what I would consider an upside-down position. That much at least I do know. Bats do not roost by perching; they hang head-down. I move him to the lampshade, which is made of burlap over a wire frame, and he hooks the claws of his feet to the lower rim. Cautiously I release my hold, and he is hanging free. "Ahhhhh," he sighs. "Better. Much better."

"Right," I say, crisp and efficient again. "Now I'm off. Not for long. Not over half an hour."

Hatted and jacketed I hurry outside and hop into my car. Seven minutes and I am at a pet store. Eight minutes more and I have made my purchase. Nine more (a tangle at a traffic light) and I am back home. Twenty-four minutes.

He is there, hanging motionless, wings folded about him. His eyes are closed, but they open as I come in and watch me as I shed hat and jacket and ease down into the chair. I open the small container I have bought. It is fairly full of pale-brownish, smooth-skinned worms, the larvae of certain beetles that infest grain products and whose scientific name I have never bothered to learn. Out of the catchall drawer in my desk comes a pair of eyebrow tweezers I use to extract splinters from my hands after attempts at amateur carpentry. With them I pick up one of the worms and offer it to him.

He seems to recoil a bit. "What is that thing?" he says.

"A mealworm," I say. "Cage birds are said to dote on them. A red-jacketed book over there on a shelf is a standard authority on bats. The author states he once introduced a bat, one of your own species, to mealworms, and that bat found them delicious."

Cautiously he takes one end of the worm between his small but well-equipped jaws. Cautiously he closes on it so that his teeth penetrate and the interior juices flow into his mouth. I could swear that a look of pleased surprise appears on his small face. The rest of the mealworm disappears into his mouth and he chews vigorously.

"Very good," says the Bat. "Very good indeed. The taste is vaguely familiar. At some time or another I must have dined on some of these when they had become adult beetles and taken to flight. I hope you have a good supply."

I keep count of the tweezer trips between container and mouth before he shakes his head to signify enough. Twenty-one. Considering his size, a considerable dinner. Or rather, considering the time of day, a considerable breakfast or brunch. Meanwhile I believe he is beginning to regard me, not as before simply with respect, now in distinct friendship. I must be right, as his next words indicate.

"A friend in need," he says. "You know the rest of that saying. I heard it occasionally where I used to live but never really understood it until now. That was in the attic of a ranger's cabin where I spent many a daytime and even hibernated several winters. Many an interesting conversation I overheard from below me in the cabin. If I speak well, as I like to think I do, it is because I try to copy that ranger. A college man. Even a graduate degree, I believe.

He spent some of his time studying the habits of ground squirrels."

"He should have been studying you," I say. "Much more fascinating a subject."

"Really, sir?" says the Bat. "I disagree. All creatures are equally interesting, each in his own way. For myself, well, we bats dislike speaking or thinking ill of anyone. We believe in cooperation or at least tolerance among all creatures—except, of course, where the predator-prey relationship holds. The principle there is simple, but its application can become rather complex. All of us living creatures are either predator or prey and often both. I prey on insects. There are other creatures who would like to prey on me. Many an owl, for example, has tried to make a meal of me. If one should—I assure you that would be only if I failed to be vigilant and execute adequate evasive maneuvers—I would not blame him. I would not like it, but I would not blame him any more than I hope any insect I catch blames me. But why do you think me, by which I hope you mean all bats, to be so fascinating?"

"Because you can fly," I say.

"Oh, that," he says. "Well, yes, it is a distinction. But unique with us bats only among mammals. In some ways actually a limitation. To have our wings we have had to sacrifice other uses of our arms and hands and to some extent even of our legs. As a result we have difficulty when grounded. More accurately, *if* grounded, because for most of us that happens only by mishap as it did to me early this morning. On the ground we bats can walk or try to run only in a ludicrous scrambling, crawling, hip-hopping manner. We have freedom of movement only in the air. Which reminds me that I think I now have enough strength to do a bit of flying. My metabolism is rapid, you know. That food is already working in me. I need some rest in more appropriate surroundings. Does that fireplace in that corner have a damper?"

"No," I say, "Why do you ask?"

"It will take me a while," he says, "to recuperate fully from my recent ordeal. One, perhaps two, light-dark cycles should suffice. That fireplace, provided you build no fires in it, could provide excellent quarters. I require a roosting place cooler than this room but not too cold. Have to lower my internal temperature some but not too much for proper resting. As an expert on fireplaces, or rather chimneys, I think about halfway up over there would be about right. Do you mind?"

"A pleasure," I say. "You are my guest. My house is your house."

"What a nice way of making one welcome," he says. "I must remember that saying. Well, here goes."

He lets go of the lampshade rim and drops, body twisting, wings unfolding fast to beat at the air. There is not enough free space, and he plumps down on his belly on the desk top.

"Oops," he says. "Not as strong as I thought." He moves toward the desk edge, and his shuffling hippety-hopping is a silly-seeming gait. He reaches the edge and pushes out into the air. I am afraid he will thump to the floor—but no, in the last fraction of a second that thirteen-inch wingspan buoys him and he is airborne. Wasting no strength, he swoops straight to the fireplace and tilts up to land against the back wall, clutching with the small thumb-claws jutting just above his wings at holds in the soot-encrusted firebricks.

His voice comes faintly to me. "All right now." Listening intently, I hear the tiny scritches as he backs upward, using the five bigger claws on each foot. Then silence. Somewhere up the chimney he has found a congenial temperature and a good roosting spot, has taken firm hold with his foot-claws and dropped down to hang in his proper resting position.

Evening of the same day. I have thought of him often over there in the fireplace chimney, but not now for an hour or more. In the mail this afternoon were galley proofs of my latest book. I have been checking through these, sometimes amused, sometimes irritated, by certain suggestions marring the margins and made by an overly conscientious copy editor who is addicted to use of a brown pencil. I have black-penciled pointed retorts to some of these on some of those margins. At the moment I am considering another.

"Heigh-ho, sir," says the Bat. "I am feeling much better."

Before I can even try to locate him he is much in evidence, swooping in a circle around my head and off toward the farthest corner of the room. He is there, he is here, he is everywhere, high and low and round about, performing what seem to me astounding aerial gymnastics. Then he comes in fast and coasts with wings outstretched like a fan around the lampshade, almost touching it, and glides on up to a perfect two-point landing on one of the drapes framing the window near me.

"Wow!" I say. "That was quite an exhibition!"

"Only a bit of exercise," he says. "Nothing fancy. I find I am in fair shape but tire rather quickly. Just a matter of time building up more strength. And this room rather cramps my style. A trifle confining for my type of flying. You should see what one of the little fast fellows, say a pipistrelle, could do in here. He could zoom into a ceiling corner, do a triple somersault without touching anything, and be back out munching a mosquito."

"Is it true," I say, "that they—you, too, of course—could do it in the dark?"

"Certainly, sir," he says. "What has light or dark to do with it? Actually, perhaps even better in the dark. Fewer sight distractions to hamper flight concentration."

"So I have it straight from the horse's mouth," I say, "that you bats do navigate by a form of sonar, by echolocation."

"Certainly we do," he says. "Though I am not exactly flattered to be referred to as a horse. All of us bats depend on our sonar to some extent, most of us almost entirely. It is more accurate than eyesight, which is of little use anyway at night. Sonar we need, and sonar we have. Would you like a demonstration? You could turn out that light and close those drapes and I . . ."

"No need," I say. "I believe you."

"Right, sir," he says. "You could not hear me anyway. My signals are much too fast for your ears and much too high a frequency. Do you happen to have on hand any more of those—those—what did you call them? Mealworms?"

By way of reply I open a drawer and take out the container, open it, set it on the desk. I am reaching for the catchall drawer when his voice stops me.

"Sir. Please. No tweezers. I am not an infant. No more hand-feeding. It could weaken my self-respect."

A simple glide down and he is on the desk by the container. "Interesting," he says. "I am deliberately grounding myself." Propping himself up just enough with his wings, he stretches his head forward to take a worm—and stops.

"Perhaps I should explain," he says. "I have no desire to overtax your hospitality. This is my reasoning: if I should go on out that chimney and forage for myself, with the weather as it still is the hunting would be poor, and I would probably obtain only enough food to sustain life, not to build up strength. By accepting your generosity I can recuperate more rapidly."

"My food is your food," I say.

"A neat paraphrase," he says. "Now if you will excuse me."

I watch him eating, a small part of my mind keeping count again, the rest pondering the paradox he presents. A moment ago, in flight, he was a vision of vibrant life, of activity under perfect control and precision. Now, there on the desk, he appears awkward and handicapped. Why? Because he is out of his element. We tend to think of the myriad taxonomic class of the birds, who are alien to us in many ways, and the even more myriad insects, who are even more alien to us, as the masters of the medium of the air. They are. But so is he, as much and perhaps more so. Barring accidents, he can live out his entire life without ever being grounded as he is right now. We other mammals are earthbound. He alone among us is not. His seeming grotesqueness when grounded is a badge of honor. He is unique among us.

There is a flicker of movement. With an awkward hopping and sudden flurry of wings he is lifting off the desk, swinging around the room, landing on the drape again. That small part of my mind tucks away the fact that the count this time has been twenty-five mealworms.

"A repast to remember," says the Bat. "My gratitude is in proportion. But you have such a serious, thinking look on your face. May I inquire whether something puzzles you?"

"Yes," I say. "I am wondering about the how and the why of your amazing flight and navigation skills. How and why you achieved them. I believe I know the how. Like the so-called flying squirrels, who do not really fly but simply glide, you originally led arboreal lives aloft in trees and evolved membranes that stretched out from your body to your limbs to facilitate gliding. Those squirrels seem to have been content to stop there—unless, being younger creatures than you in an evolutionary sense, in a few more million years they too go on to true flight. You seem to have been determined from a very early start to conquer the air. A tough job. As an early mammal you were committed to four-legged locomotion and to fur not feathers, which are invaluable aids to the birds. You had to make a difficult array of anatomical changes in yourself. Why did you do it?"

"I could sum an answer," says the Bat, "by stating that my—or rather our, since I am speaking for all bats—cooperative nature was responsible. But before I go into that, let me assert that I doubt the so-called flying squirrels will ever try to, even want to, achieve true flight. They are primarily vegetarians, dining chiefly on nuts and fruits and such. Tree products. Their gliding helps them get from tree to tree and to evade possible predators. They have no need for true flight. We bats, originally insectivores, insect-eaters, and most of us remaining so though you humans have kindly given us our own taxonomic order, are in a different category. Insects, a vast number of them, fly. We fly to prey on them. You might say we do most of our food shopping in the air."

"But the other insectivores," I say, "those we include in the order Insectivora, the shrews and moles and hedgehogs and tenrecs, do very well without flying."

"Of course," he says. "That is precisely my point. They do a good job of insect-eating on the ground, underground, and above ground in bushes and trees. They need no assistance—or, for that matter, competition—from us bats. Way back in the early years we bats noted that our class, the mammals, was neglecting one field of insect-eating endeavor and a vast field at that. The realm of the air. Even then it was apparent that the insects, unless constantly checked, could dominate the world. We bats decided, in effect we volunteered, to extend control into that previously neglected field. As you suggest, that was a difficult assignment at first. But it has had its compensations, as cooperative efforts and willingness to take on hard tasks always have in the long run. The field of the air has been wonderfully fertile for our feeding through the ages. Working in it, we bats did long ago what you humans have done only recently, spread throughout virtually the entire habitable world. And there has been what I regard as a bonus, a reward. True flight, once achieved, has its own special joys and exhilaration."

"I am sure it does," I say. "I know a few pilots who have the same feeling about flying."

"Pilots?" he says. "Pilots? Oh, yes, I have heard the word. You mean humans who steer those ungainly things you call airplanes. That is a form of flying, at least moving—or, rather, being carried—through the air without contact with the ground. Primarily just a means of getting from here to there and adequate for that purpose. Awkward things, however, imprisoning their passengers in order to carry them. Requiring ground crews to keep them functional and an elaborate subsidiary system to supply them with fuel. Inefficient, really, except in the matter of straightaway speed. It would be amusing to see one of them try to capture a nimble insect in flight, have to change course five times in one second, double back instantly on itself, turn a swift side-slipping somersault—and nab that insect in its tail. But I should not have said that. I told you we bats dislike speaking ill of anyone or anything. Some of you humans do quite enough of that about us bats. Oooops! I am doing it again. Forgive me."

"No forgiveness needed," I say. "Like so many of my kind I used to think because your flight often seems so erratic and fluttery that you bats are poor bumbling flyers. Only recently have I learned what amazing agility and control you are really displaying."

"Thank you, sir," says the Bat. "That comes close to being flattery. But as I said a while ago, I find I tire easily. I am tired now. May I ask yet another favor?"

"My favors are your favors," I say, adding a chuckle. I am almost certain I hear a tiny gurgle from him that could be a similar response.

"Wonderful things, words," he says. "They can convey delightful shades of meaning. I go deeper into your debt. Thus, there is a fair supply of those mealworms remaining. There is also a brick in that fireplace a short way up which protrudes just enough to be a small shelf. If you

would set that container on it, I could have snacks now
and again with rests between and thereby hasten my full
recovery."

"Ingenious," I say and reach to tilt the lampshade so
that light shines toward the fireplace corner. I take the
container, leaving it open of course, and go over and kneel
down and poke my head in the opening. Right enough, a
patch of darker shadow that must be the protruding brick.
I place the container on it. Right again, just enough room
to hold it. As I pull back there is a swish past me and he is
landing on the back of the fireplace and starting to crawl
up.

"Wait," I say. "You have not told me why you are
working your way south."

"No, no, no," he says. "Not now, sir. I am trying not to
think about that. Fretting over it could delay my recovery."

He is out of sight now. I hear a few faint scritches. Then
nothing.

Evening of the next day. Spring has begun to obey the
calendar. I have been busy, running a few errands, working
in my garden. Now I am checking through the final sheets
of galley proofs.

Occasionally through the day I have thought of him
there in the fireplace. Twice I have poked my head in the
opening to peer up. Each time, in the dim light filtering
down from the upper opening, I have seen or been reasonably sure I have seen him about halfway up, apparently
sound asleep. But now I am wondering all over again what
has happened to him. I peered up again just before sitting
down at the desk, this time using a flashlight, and he was

not there. The container was empty and tumbled to the base of the fireplace. But he was gone. I am vaguely annoyed, feeling that he has somehow failed what I thought was a genuine friendship. And he has made one of my errands a waste of time.

Humph. That copy editor has done it again, insisted on wanting to follow the technical distinction between "that" and "which" however much it would offend the mental ear in this particular sentence. I will black-pencil the brown-penciling. I do so.

"Heigh-ho and a thousand thanks," says the Bat, zooming from the fireplace to the window drape near me.

I stare up at him.

"Well fueled and fully recovered," he says. "Proved by experimental flight three times around your house at good speed, weaving in and out around the pillars of the portal. Thanks to you, sir, I am ready to be on my way."

"If I moved fast myself," I say, "I might beat you to that fireplace and block it and have you trapped in here."

"Nonsense, sir," he says. "That is not in character with your previous behavior. Impossible too. I have noted there are two other chimneys indicating two other fireplaces in two other rooms. You could not beat me to all three. But whatever for?"

"To keep you here," I say, "until you tell me why you want to go south."

"Of course I will tell you," he says, "now that I am thinking of my mission again. But only briefly. I am behind what I hoped would be my schedule."

"Brief will do," I say.

"As you probably know," says the Bat, "we bats are worldwide in distribution. What you probably do not

know is that we have a worldwide system of communication, bat to bat across the spaces, which can be used when
needed. We use it only for matters of real importance and,
of course, between continents only in absolute emergen-
cies. During recent decades there have been scattered but
disquieting rumors of declines in bat populations in many
regions. Last year it became known that this is not only a
worldwide development but also is particularly serious
here in North America. A decision was made to devote the
coming year, now this year, to the gathering of data in an
attempt to determine causes and assess the situation."

"That," I say, "I certainly did not know. It sounds as if
you have something similar to our human United Nations
organization, which has branches supposed to do that kind
of work for us."

"No doubt," he says. "It is the logical way to attack any
problem affecting all or a goodly portion of one's kind. But
I proceed to my part in the survey. We *Eptesicus* bats have
a range covering most of North America and have volunteered to conduct the survey throughout that range. Western headquarters in the Denver area. I am a courier head-
ing south as far as the Mexican border to alert fellow
brown bats along the way. Then I will retrace my course
garnering what data they have discovered."

"Do you have any ideas as yet," I say, "of what the
results will be?"

"No," he says. "I have been too much a carefree flit-
about during my seven years of life to date to do any
thinking about it. That is why I flew forward to enlist as a
courier. Sort of making amends. Moreover, accurate data
can be obtained only if one has no preconceived notions
that might hamper impartial judgment. There. I have told

you. Now I must be on my way. But you have over-
whelmed me with your care and generosity. How can I
ever repay you?"

"Ah," I reply. "My generosity was not a simple gift. The
meals and shelter were actually a bribe. I want you to
promise that you will stop off here on your return trip and
give me a report."

"Certainly I will," he says. "You have more than earned
it. My word as a bat. Now I really must go."

"If you must, you must," I say, "but no climbing up a
chimney. You shall leave as you first came here, through a
door."

He is talking as I carry him outside. "So this is the way I
first arrived in what you so kindly say is my house. Very
appropriate to be leaving the same way."

I face south. Gently I toss him into the air, and that
thirteen-inch wingspan spreads and beats in the swim-
ming motion that is a bat's way of flying, and he is rising at
an angle southward.

"Bon voyage!" I call out.

Faintly I believe I hear him: " . . . is a friend indeed."
Already he is a dark spot merging into the darkness of the
night sky. No erratic twists and turns, no aerial gymnastics. No need for them. He is fueled with my mealworms.
He is flying straight and true, off on his batkind mission.

Time passes. Spring has eased into summer, and summer has reached its middle mark. I need consult no calendar to know that. The Chinese elms hereabouts, which
start the season with bright new green leaves, now have
the skimpy worried look which regularly by midsummer
has been inflicted upon them. Their leaves are riddled,

many of them mere skeletons. Myriad elm beetle larvae have been at work on those leaves, and mature beetles are currently harassing my wife, infesting the house, leaving yellow spots on our curtains, some even managing to get into our refrigerator.

I have little sympathy for those elm trees, not alone because by supplying the elm beetle diet they are responsible for the beetle invasion. They have their own nuisance quota. I understand why they are know as "Tingley's folly." They acquired a strong expanding foothold in the area some decades ago when one Tingley (a onetime state governor, I believe), in a burst of misguided enthusiasm, obtained thousands of seedlings which were handed out gratis to residents who would plant them. Now it is only too well known that they develop prodigious root systems which compete only too successfully with more genteel trees and which continue to send up shoots all around after the originals have been cut down. Moreover, they produce seeds in numbers to match the beetles, and these seeds spread everywhere and instantly start sprouting with particular fondness for gardens.

Midsummer. Thoughts of my brown bat friend have dwindled, and for a week or more I have not even wondered what may have happened to him. That is, until right now, this evening, this late evening. A bit earlier I had been thinking about elm trees and elm beetles and a new pesticide which is supposed to be bad for beetles. Now, before going to bed, I have been looking through previously unread portions of the morning paper. Back at breakfast time I had read only what I consider to be the most important items in any newspaper, the front-page headlines, the comic strips, and the columnists' comments on the editorial page. Just now, tucked away on an inside page, I have come upon an item about bats, about the Carlsbad bats. Carlsbad. Down south there in the state in the general area of my bat friend's mission.

I lean back in my executive's chair, thinking of him. There has been heavy mortality among the Carlsbad bats, noted at last even by us humans for the typically human reason that the bats have been a major tourist attraction at the Carlsbad Caverns and the attraction has lost its attractiveness. How about my friend? Poor fellow. He too must have succumbed to whatever is sowing death among bats down that way. Or perhaps he never even made it that far south. Or perhaps again he did—and fell by the wayside on his return trip. Otherwise before now he certainly would have completed his mission.

I close my eyes, trying to remember him as last I saw him, winging southward.

"Sir!"

I open my eyes. He is there, on the drape, upside-down in what is rightside-up roosting for him.

"You're alive!" I say. "You made it! Welcome, welcome. My house is your house."

"It is not," says the Bat. "It is your house. I want no part of it." There is a sternness, an edge almost of anger, in his voice. "The temptation was strong," he says, "to pass on by, ignoring you. But I gave my word as a bat."

"For heaven's sake!" I say. "What's got into you? What have I done?"

"You?" he says. "I do not know about you as an individual. Perhaps you have done nothing. Nothing except being a human. Which to my present mind is quite enough. The evidence is not all in, and perhaps there are other factors, but my mind is made up about the major factor. Even what others there are may be human-connected."

"Whatever are you talking about?" I say.

"I promised you a report," he says. "I will make one. Even though that means speaking ill of your kind to your face."

"Go ahead," I say. "I offer my own promise. That my friendship will hold."

"Perhaps," says the Bat. "Perhaps not. That is immaterial. I keep my word, omitting any account of my travels and contacts, citing only in logical sequence the results that are becoming ever more apparent. First: rumors of declines in bat populations are not rumors, they are flagrant facts. Second: declines are particularly noticeable in areas infested by humans. Third: this is not necessarily related to the number of humans occupying a specific area. That is, the bat mortality rate in the vicinity of cities and towns, places where humans congregate in large numbers, is only slightly higher than it has been during recent decades. Fourth: there is increasing evidence that bat mortality is highest with the rate rising in those areas in which humans carry on a specific activity, an increasingly widespread activity. You call it agriculture. Not the harvesting of natural food supplies but the deliberate raising of food crops."

My mind flips back to my earlier thoughts about elm beetles and the possible control of them. "Ah, yes," I say. "I think I begin. . ."

"No interruptions, please," says the Bat. "Let me proceed. The connection between human agriculture and bat mortality became ever more obvious to me as I gathered data. But the explanation eluded me until several enterprising comrades made some daytime patrols. They reported what we bats, active only at night, had not noted before, that you humans use strange devices to spray noxious materials on your trees and over your fields."

"Ah, yes," I say again. "Pesticides. Insecticides."

"Exactly," says the Bat. "I took to daylight patrolling myself. I roosted in sheds and barns, and I listened to humans talking. And I learned. Insecticides. Poisons to kill insects. The effect: poisoning of the food of us bats."

"Ah, yes, yes, yes," I say. "I had not thought of that in relation to you bats. But even we humans have noted the effect on birds. You might have found your explanation by consulting some of them."

"Impossible," says the Bat. "Birds are not mammals. They are too alien to us for any real communication. But I feel more kindly toward them now that you tell me they too suffer the grief."

"But wait," I say. "You bats do not eat dead insects. You catch them alive in the air. Most of you anyway. Do you mean that the insecticides reduce your food supplies so drastically that you suffer from malnutirition and starvation?"

"No, no, no," says the Bat. "No doubt our food supplies are diminished by your insecticides. That merely means that we have to forage farther and more diligently. The reproductive powers of insects are beyond calculation. They can be moderately controlled, not eliminated. No. The effect of your pesticides on us bats is much more insidious and deadly. Inevitably we eat some insects contaminated by a poison who have not yet succumbed to it or have not absorbed enough of it from their plant feeding to kill them. The residues of that poison remain in us and accumulate. Rarely enough to kill an adult bat. But— but—it is difficult for me to go on."

"Please," I say. "Tell me. I must know."

A clearly audible sigh comes from him. "Apparently the poisons accumulated in a mother bat's body, while not enough to bother her overmuch, in some way enter into the milk which her baby draws from her breast. That baby is born, presumably happy and healthy. But as its feeding times pass, poison accumulates in its young body, more than it can tolerate. In time it fares forth on its own first flight and—and it—it cannot sustain strength and coordination. Despite frantic efforts it cannot make its way back to the roost. At last it falls to the ground to die a lingering death."

He sighs again and seems to shake himself into going on. "In more extreme cases, after only a day or two of nursing the baby sickens, it weakens, it can no longer cling to its mother's fur and it—it too—falls to the cave floor and dies."

"Horrible," I say. "Are you certain that is what happens?"

"I have been where the evidence is conclusive," says the Bat. "I have seen. All my life I have heard of the bats of the Carlsbad Caverns, my relatives of the Molossidae family, the freetail bats who have lived there from time immemorial, in their millions, superb flyers, far foragers, setting examples of cooperative communal living for all other creatures. I have seen the human agriculture that is spreading through much of their foraging range, a great deal of it made possible by irrigation. I have been in the caverns and talked to freetails who still survive. And there in the caverns I have seen—oh, sir, what heart-wrenching sights. This has been the birth season. Bodies of babies lying on the cave floor, some still faintly struggling. And—and—I saw—I saw more of them fall."

"Good God in his heaven!" I say. "Shades of Cambodia and Vietnam."

We are silent, the Bat and I. His voice is first to break the silence. "Your last words mean nothing to me," he says.

It is my turn to sigh. "I refer," I say, "to two countries where the human situation has been roughly and tragically similar, particularly in regard to babies and young children. But the poisons at work there are of a different nature. They are inherent in us humans. We are self-poisoners."

I doubt he has heard me. He is thinking his own thoughts. "Do you know, sir," he says, "I feel better now that I have told you, have put into words what has been in my mind. Perhaps not better, only different. Anger has been in me, and I do not like being angry. It is subsiding in me, giving way to sorrow. And new thoughts are pushing forward, thoughts crowded by the impact of my experiences. Emotion has been clouding my perception of facts. Considering now as impartially as I can the data I have gathered, seeking only the truth, I note there is no evidence that you humans, using your insecticides, do so with deliberate intent to harm us bats. You are simply waging a kind of war against the insects. The effect on us is a bitter sideline result probably unforeseen."

"Unforeseen," I say, "because unconsidered, no thought given to it. And when such side effects do become known to us humans, as recently in regard to birds, not much is done to redress the error. We ban a particular pesticide and develop another to take its place—and then in time new effects appear. It is an endless ironic cycle."

"But why?" says the Bat. "Insect control is not such a difficult matter. Through long ages we bats with the able assistance of the ground-based insectivores—and, yes, the birds—have kept a reasonable balance of control. And in their turn various plants have developed insect-repellents to protect themselves, and many have learned to group varieties of species for mutual protection. Why have you humans resorted to pesticide warfare?"

"Because of our own reproductive ability," I say, "plus our scientific advances lowering infant mortality and reducing diseases and extending life-spans. That combination has created an ever-expanding human population requiring an ever-expanding food supply. Add to that our kind of agriculture, which we believe is the only kind that can meet our food demands. One-crop agriculture. Vast fields, whole areas, stripped of other plant life (and thus of most if not all animal life too) and devoted to one single crop at a time. Each such field is a paradise for insects that feed on its particular crop. We have created ideal conditions for them, bountiful food with most if not all natural checks and repellents abolished. Because of our imperative need we cannot tolerate even partial destruction of the crop as a toll, a tax, levied by the insects. We must try to destroy as many as possible of those insects. We cannot, or will not because it is inefficient, attack them individually, one at a time, as you bats do, so we seek to scatter destruction wholesale among them."

"Strange," says the Bat. "At the same time you are destroying so many of us other creatures who are actually your helpers in insect control."

"Yes," I say. "But we are hooked into that system. I can try experiments in my little garden, shunning pesticides, encouraging insect enemies of the insect pests, mixing plants that mutually repel each other's pests, even using certain flowers which yield no food but do discourage certain insects. Yet the commercial farmer who is no longer really a farmer but a businessman with a big capital investment in equipment cannot do the same on the scale on which he operates—or thinks he cannot, and probably he is right. We humans need the crop which with the aid of insecticides he raises. We are hooked."

"I follow your explanation," says the Bat, "though I must add that it seems to me to be species-selfish and in the overall view actually wasteful. In protecting the food supply of your single species you are curtailing and poisoning that of us bats and all other insect-eaters."

"Right," I say. "But, as you have said, not deliberately. Virtually by accident. Another factor involved is the increasing specialization of our scientists and technologists. So much detailed knowledge has been amassed that each can be efficient only in his narrowed-down portion of a portion of the discipline in which he works. Consider this in simplistic terms in regard to pesticides. Insects damage our crops. A researcher sets to work to develop something that will kill those insects without harming the plants and without harming (if we are careful) humans who eat the plants. Those restrictions define the path for his research. Side effects are not his immediate problem and are outside of his portion of a portion of his discipline. He achieves an effective pesticide. With it we humans can kill those insects in satisfying numbers. We do so. Later we learn we are also killing many other creatures against whom we have no cause for animosity — gratitude and friendship, actually. But that researcher is not responsible individually for what has happened. He did his job well, reached the goal set for him. And well, yes, we other humans were in too much of a hurry to use his pesticide to encourage other specialists in other disciplines to investigate other aspects of that pesticide's potentialities. That pattern of leaping before looking, of seizing apparent advantage without considering possible disadvantages, is ingrained in human behavior."

"Your pardon, sir," says the Bat. "I accept your explanation—but not the attitude that goes with it. You are not only pessimistic, you are fatalistic. You speak as if the dire things we are discussing simply are and must be. That is a defeatist attitude. I do not now know any answers, any solutions. I do know that none can be found when such an attitude prevails. Another new thought is pushing up in my mind, but I hesitate to state it. Is your friendship holding?"

"Not only holding," I say, "but strengthened by my regret at what my kind are doing to your kind."

"I think," says the Bat, "that except perhaps for an occasional rare individual you humans have let yourselves be handicapped by the fact that you cannot fly, that you are ground-bound, confined primarily to a one-level, two-dimensional existence. You have minds marvelous in many ways, but you permit them to be limited by that limitation. Lacking the habits of thought that are fostered by the freedom, the three-dimensional, virtually all-dimensional freedom, of flight, you tend to think only in straight lines, from this point to that point on the one level and by the most direct path. Your minds aim at a goal and move toward it as if confined in a tunnel, unwilling or at least unaccustomed to winging off along the way into other directons and dimensions with their possibly related possibilities and contingent effects."

"Whew!" I say. "That thought of yours is certainly winging off in a new direction."

"Do not give me overmuch credit," says the Bat. "As the only flying mammals, we bats have the mind-habit of winging-off thinking. But I have been using abstract phrases and big words. Let me try to sum this in simpler manner. As you suggest, too often it is only with hindsight, after a mistake is made or damage done, that you humans try to take into account possibilities and contingencies overlooked before. My thought is that, unable bodily to fly, inexperienced in flight, only a few of you ever and most of you never let the one part of you which can fly, your thoughts, take wing and explore and assess in the realm of the possibles beyond the scope of one-level, two-dimensional existence."

"That is a generous thought," I say. "I would like to believe in it. You are suggesting it is not incapacity on the part of us humans which produces the problems we are discussing, but more accurately a carelessness, a failure to use more fully the intelligence we possess. As you put this, we have a habit of mind that perhaps we could change if we really wanted to, if we put our minds to it. A generous thought. But, alas, it seems to me that the whole record of human activity to date proves otherwise."

"Your pardon again, sir," says the Bat, and I can almost believe there is a tenderness in his tone. "You are indulging in that habit right now. Your mind is in a tunnel, moving in a limited straight line, concentrating solely on those things which point toward the pessimistic goal you think that tunnel must lead to. Let your thoughts take wing, have the freedom of flight. My own mind was in a tunnel when I stopped here tonight. Talking to you with your friendship holding has set it free again. For my part I have faith in you humans. The true capacity of your intelligence is virtually unlimited. How else could you relative newcomers to this ancient Earth, you late additions to the mammalian roster, so quickly have become the dominant life-form of the whole class? In a sense you are still mere youngsters making the hasty unthinking mistakes of youth. I have faith that in the long run you will uphold the honor of the mammalian brotherhood, will restore and maintain this world as a better homeland for all of us."

"I wish I could have the same faith," I say, "but doubts weigh heavy in my mind."

"Doubts have value as warnings," says the Bat. "Simply add to them hope and give wings to your mind. And now I really must be on my way. I suspect that as soon as we couriers have reported, we bats will be busy using our worldwide communications network to determine what areas around the Earth are safest for our survival through these tough times and until conditions improve. I hope to be helpful. And now I find a spot of sentiment in me. One last favor. I should like to leave your house, which I accept again as my house, carried once more in your hand. Somehow that seems a symbol for the future."

He leaves the drape and circles the room and lands lightly on my outstretched hand. Carefully I carry him out into the front yard and face northward. Gently I toss him into the air, and those wide-spanned wings unfold and he is airborne.

"Farewell," I say. "I mean that in the original meaning of the word, that you fare well."

He checks his forward flight, executes a looping reversal, and swings in a fluid arc to make a four-point landing on my right shoulder. "A thought," he says, "has just winged up in my mind. That sometime in the still-dim future a grandchild of mine many times removed will be able to say to a grandchild of yours many times removed, 'Heigh-ho, sir and friend. My ancestor was right.'"

I feel the slight pressure on my shoulder as he makes an awkward little leap for a takeoff and his wings open, and on the instant he is a graceful being again, in his element, free in the all-dimensional freedom of the air. He rises upward, seeking altitude, and heads northward into distance to complete his courier mission.

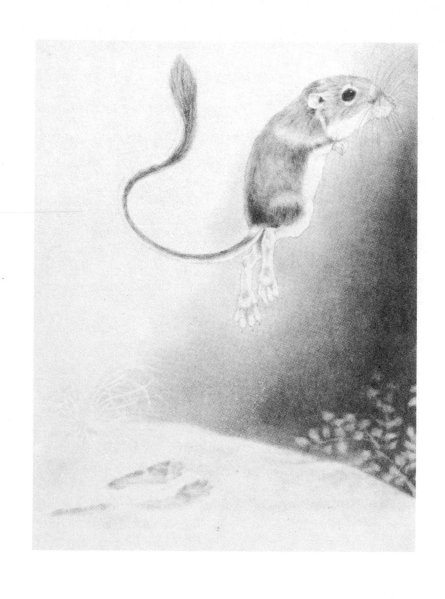

. . . and a Kangaroo Rat

(Dipodomys ordii)

THE IRRIGATION DITCH known as the Pueblo Lateral which skirts one side of our acre-and-a-half of river valley land was dug and side-mounded quite a while ago, well before we humans multiplied hereabouts and began subdividing the land grants of the early settlement years. The ditch follows the original contour of the region with a fine disregard for compass readings and the human obsession with straight lines and precise north-south east-west boundaries. So doing, it slices off a fat corner of our property which otherwise would be a neat square two-acre plot.

Across the ditch the straight-line obsession reasserts

itself. Result: a right triangle with two sides defined by
fence, hypotenuse by the ditch, a seeming no-man's-land.
Some of this is part of the conservancy district right-of-
way and the rest must belong, by human reckoning, to
someone or some governmental body. For all apparent
purposes, however, it is simply a piece of wasteland, subject to human activity only occasionally when some
walker or jogger or neighborhood kid on a horse passes
along the decrepit almost-abandoned bridle path that follows the ditch.

Sand and silt cleaned out of the ditch each spring by a
conservancy crew and thrown up on the west bank has
blown out over that triangle in layers through the years,
banking some against the fence lines, creating an area of
deep loose soil that for lack of moisture (ironic, this, with
ditch water flowing past eight months of the year)
nourishes only sparse scattered vegetation: some clumps
of native grasses, a few scraggly cacti, in spring a smatter-
ing of swift ephemeral wildflowers, and an interesting
variety of annual weeds whose brown carcasses drift in
winter against the fences and help keep the triangle a
small isolated world of its own—a small piece of typical,
almost-desert southwest sitting serene in the midst of the
semi-urban outskirts of Albuquerque.

I used to stand by our own fence paralleling the ditch
and look out at that triangle of unused real estate and
think to myself: what a fine homesite for one of the
Dipodomys tribe, a kangaroo rat. Now no more. I stand by
our fence, looking over. But I do no such thinking. He is
there.

This morning I went out through our side gate and along
the ditch to purloin a dead tree branch, blown down by last

night's wind, which eventually I will saw into firewood. I saw his tracks. Longish marks in wind-smoothed sand that could have been made by some miniature skier hopping on his runners. But no skier would have claws on the front ends of his runners leaving scritch-marks in the sand. And I found an entrance to his burrow, likely just one of the several he has or will have as he adds chambers and storerooms and hidden escape hatches to his underground headquarters. And again, conclusive evidence, as I bend down to peer into that burrow doorway, I heard him thumping with his long hindfeet on their long hindlegs his recognition of my presence and his emphatic pronouncement: Occupied! No trespassing! Go away!

And so, what I am thinking now is that somehow out of somewhere we have acquired a new neighbor and that, since he is nocturnal in habits, I will have to wait until nightfall to get a glimpse of him and, with luck, to make his acquaintance.

*   *   *

Evening. A nicely dark night, its darkness eased only by starlight with a slim assist from a sliver of moon low to the western horizon. For half an hour or more I have been sitting on the ditch bank, my back to the ditch itself, silent, motionless. I tell myself to be patient and I am, time passes and my head droops in drowsiness.

An involuntary nod brings me wide awake. Something is happening out in that triangle. My eyes give me a blurred impression of swift haphazard movement by some small object behaving like a bouncing ball, while my ears catch small sounds apparently coming from here and there and everywhere. Somehow those sounds seem phonetic and they have rhythm and a repetitious pattern. I try to frame them into syllables, to see them mentally in letters. In my concentration I scarcely realize that I am murmuring aloud: *"Leh . . . tie . . . grore . . . eye . . . sore."*

"Tigers, man, tigers."

No mistaking those words, perhaps because they come in simple sequence from a single spot. Straining vision, I seek to locate that spot. Yes. There he is, about fifteen feet away, the bulgy-headed squat little shape of him sitting up on his long hindfeet and long hindlegs, no doubt braced behind by even longer tail. Alert, alive, he is looking at me.

"Tigers?" I say. "Did you mention tigers?"

"Yes, yes, of course yes," says the Kangaroo Rat. His tone is cheerful, matter-of-fact. "Yes," he says. "Tigers. Big animals. Big teeth. Big noise. In celebration tonight I have put them into my ditty for dancing. It goes like this: *Let tigers roar–I soar!* Neat, man, neat. Better than the one I used last night: *While others creep–I leap!* Yes, yes, of course yes. The tiger business is definitely better. Do you read me, man?"

"I'm not even trying," I say. "It's too incongruous. Big tigers—and tiny you."

"Tiny is as tiny does," he says. "But let me explain. I am willing to let tigers roar so fearsomely because I can soar so beautifully. I can jump, leap, soar some twenty times my body height, some thirty times my body length. I can take off at any angle, even backwards when wanted. I can change course in mid-air, pick my landing site in a split fraction of a fragment of a second. Yes, yes, of course yes. I can soar and soar but I cannot roar, just as a tiger can roar and roar but cannot soar. That makes us even in any cosmic balancing of ability counts."

"Those are rather restricted entries in the cosmic ledger," I say. "All the same, I get your point. You suggest you are celebrating. Tonight and last night. Do you do that every evening?"

"No, no, of course no," he says. "Only on special occasions. This is a special occasion. A two-night, perhaps even a three-night occasion. I celebrate my freedom, my escape from captivity and from the asininities of human stupidity."

"Now that," I say, "really requires an explanation."

"So I give it," he says. "Stupidity in conversation is one thing, simply to be expected from you humans. My current reference is to stupidity in actions—which I give you credit for avoiding right now, making no effort to catch me here in the open, which you simply could not do."

"Catch you?" I say. "I have already caught you in the one way I want, which is to carry on a conversation regardless of how much human stupidity I may display."

"Sensible," says the Kangaroo Rat. "So here is my tale—which I warn you may be as long as my tail. I was born across the river on what you call the West Mesa where weather has created fine sandy soil from the volcanic tufa thereabouts. My mother gave me a good education. Then, being a proper mother, when I was of suitable size, she kicked me out of the home burrow, telling me it was time I should be on my own as it is ordained each adult of my kind should be. Trust no one, she said, not even your brothers. Mark out your own territory and guard it. Keep plenty of food sorted into varieties in your storerooms. Keep any romance brief and businesslike and be done with it and back to your own burrow."

"Stern advice," I say. "Especially that last about romance."

"Sound advice," he says. "Dangerous to be away from
one's headquarters very long, even for romance. The world
is full of thieves. But I proceed. My mother had neglected
to teach me about traps. While improving the abandoned
burrow I had claimed, I bumbled into a trap, one of those
drop-door wire things. Some stupid scientist had set it by
one of my back exits. I say stupid in his case because he did
not want me, he wanted a prairie dog, and obviously he
was ignorant of our respective house plans. He sold me to a
pet store for three dollars. Along came another human
who bought me for ten dollars as a present for his nine-
year-old daughter, one of those silly squealing creatures
who just lo-o-o-o-o-ve animals. That was when my real
troubles began."

"They were mean to you?"

"Not mean, man. Merely stupid. They almost killed me
with kindness. You humans are weirdos. You persist in
trying to make pets of other animals without bothering to
learn about their habits, their likes and dislikes, their
dietary needs, their notions of what constitutes joy in
living. You make out fairly well with domesticated and
thus dulled animals like horses and dogs, to some extent
even with cats. In regard to others your ignorance is appal-
ling. That silly girl meant well. She figured that with my
long hindlegs I like space for action, so she had her father
make a rather large cage as cages go. Large, that is, in width
and length. But he made it low in height. If I tried even
mild soaring, I bumped my head. She figured that as a
rodent I like to scrabble in good dirt, so she put some in.
About a meagre half inch of it. Even an earthworm would

find that ridiculous. But such things were nothing to what she did about my diet."

"Surely she fed you?"

"If you could call it feeding. She tried various things, all of them horrible moist mixtures of disgusting goo. Any fool should know that my kind not only prefers but actually requires only dry foods, particularly and for example the seeds of grasses and weeds properly dried for perservation. And she polluted my cage by placing in it a container filled with that obnoxious substance known as water. Any fool should know that we never voluntarily drink water, that we shun the stuff, that we are annoyed if any of it so much as touches us. You humans actually gulp the stuff. You even take baths in it. Dust is the proper medium for bathing. A good dustbath is a good recipe not only for cleanliness but for . . ."

"Wait a moment," I say. "That water business. You must be joking. All living things need water. It's a major component of us all."

"Yes, yes, of course yes," he says. "Internally. Inside us. The point is: how does it get there? I see you need a lesson in what I could call bio-hydro-conservation. In the very act of living all of us animals, of us mammals anyway, manufacture water within us, what is called metabolic water. We synthesize it out of hydrogen from the hydrocarbons in our food and oxygen from the air. Most of all the rest of you are ridiculously spendthrift of water. You lose quantities every time you breathe the moist air out of your lungs and when you sweat, which you do much more than you realize, and again in prodigious amounts when you urinate. You waste so much that you must drink often just to stay alive. I waste not, therefore I want not. I have extra long nasal passages which I keep cooler than my lungs and thus I can condense out and retain much of what I would otherwise lose in breathing. I use a minimum of the stuff in forming my urine and concentrate this further by absorbing moisture out of it before I void it. I have other intricate techniques, but those are sufficient examples. My metabolic water meets my needs—with some assistance from the moisture in my food. Even the dryest of seeds have some. As a result, I could live out my life quite happily without so much as ever even seeing a free drop of water."

"Come now," I say. "You must be exaggerating."

"If so," he says, "only slightly. But you still have not grasped what that girl was doing to me. I rely so much on metabolic water that my organic system is tuned to the amount of moisture within me at any time. If my moisture-count is low, I feel an urge to be active, thus to step up my metabolism and produce more water within me. In a way I could say that when I was soaring a while ago, I was also giving myself a drink. But, alas, the converse is also true. Damp foodstuffs pump me full of moisture and my system, rebelling, insists that I slow down on activity, avoid producing metabolic water. I become lethargic, dulled in mind and muscle."

"Good heavens," I say. "Too much moist food and you could face a form of drowning on dry land."

"Remarkable," he says. "You have caught my meaning and put it into an exaggerated yet apt metaphor. But there is more. I ate as sparingly as I could and that silly creature thought I simply did not like what she gave me. She doubled her mistake by offering what could only be worse under the circumstances. Deadly stuff. Lettuce."

"Well, yes. Fresh lettuce certainly is chockfull of moisture."

"And it's green," he says.

"Green? What has color to do with all this?"

"Plenty," he says. "Any fool ought to know that my kind nibbles fresh green vegatation only at certain times, primarily in the spring. It contains estrogenic substances that encourage the sex urge in us. Can your mind grasp the enormity of the situation? Me, cooped alone in that cage. Nothing but lettuce in the foodline. Forced to become waterlogged internally and at the same time to suffer the pangs of unfulfillable romantic urgings. It had become a time for heroic measures."

"If what you say is true," I say, "it certainly had. I take it you took them."

"You can bet on that, baby," says the Kangaroo Rat. "I pushed myself to them. I dabbled a forehand in that repugnant water and splashed some on myself. I rolled in that meagre dirt and let some stick to my fur. I huddled down, looking as miserable as I felt. That worked. That silly girl thought I needed, even wanted, a bath. A WATER-bath. She brought a basin of the stuff and set it down by the cage. She opened the cage door—she was always cautious about that—and slipped a hand in. I stayed limp and let her pick me up. The instant the hand holding me was withdrawn out the door, I bit a finger—just a nip not a bite because she meant well—and kicked with my strong hindlegs and she squealed one of her prize squeals and dropped me. My moisture-count was high so I was somewhat wobbly, but the thought of that basin of waiting water gave me strength and I soared all over that room, what they called the kitchen. A nasty cat who had spent too much time too often staring at me in the cage got into the act. Had I been in good shape, I might have tried making him dizzy trying to figure my jumps, maybe given him a good thump on the head from an unexpected angle, but I had to get out of there. High on one jump I saw a window over the sink open about four inches. I made it up and over and out in one splendid soaring, ending in a hunched dive, and I made tracks fast and far apart till I was hidden in a clump of bushes."

He pauses, perhaps out of breath from that last burst of talk.

"And then?" I say.

"And then I waited and rested while the warm daytime air dried me towards a proper moisture-count. I waited until nighttime which is the right time for a sensible person to be about. I scouted for quite a distance around. A poor neighborhood, this whole area. Infested by too many of you humans with your endless ways of ruining good land. At last I met a pocket gopher. Fine fellows, pocket gophers. Brothers to my kind, you might say, in the pocket-possessing fraternity with similar, sensible territorial and social habits. I didn't exactly meet him, merely heard him working away underground and called down his nearest tunnel. Refreshingly grouchy and grumbly he was. Told me about this place across the ditch from his own domain just to get rid of me. So here I am with my own kingdom. Perfect in every way and all mine—except for occasional trespassers like you."

"Not a trespasser," I say. "A neighbor making a friendly visit. You can trust me."

"Yes, yes, of course yes," he says. "So you say. But trust no one, said my mother. I don't trust you. I merely tolerate you."

"Go on," I say. "You've enjoyed talking about yourself."

"In moderation," he says. "But you interrupted my special-occasion soaring. I need to finish with special twists and mid-air somersaults. Then a bit of food-gathering, say four pockets-full. I might even try a new ditty which has occurred to me: *The dryest of seeds— meet all my needs.* No. Tigers are for tonight. Prove your friendship. Go away. I dislike an audience. It cramps my style."

Obediently I go. But notions for other evenings and a whole crop of questions are sprouting in my mind.

*   ★   ★

Another evening, the very next. If he has decided on a three-night celebration, this being the third, I want to observe or at least listen. As before I sit on the ditch bank, motionless and quiet, and patience eases into drowsiness, and again, suddenly, I am wide awake and something is happening out in that triangle.

Swift blurred movement in the dimness of dark. Scattered bits of sound with their own rhythms and patterns. Obviously my hearing and/or my understanding are/is improving because I have only mild difficulty in piecing the sounds together. As before, I murmur aloud: *"What others fear—I hear."*

"Remarkable," says the Kangaroo Rat. He has stopped, is sitting up, looking at me. "You have it right. Absolutely right."

"No tigers tonight?" I say.

"No, no, of course no," he says. "I finished with them

88

last night. But certainly you can interpret tonight's ditty. It's pretty but not profound."

"Well, now," I say. "I know that you fellows have good hearing. I suppose that in some way you are referring to that."

"Slow, baby, slow," he says. "You miss the real point. Good hearing, indeed. That's damning with faint praise. We have superb hearing, the best and finest possible. From your limited perspective you may consider this noble head of mine out of proportion to my body. It is proportionately large, yes. Rightly so. It provides room for my bountiful bullae, my inner ears, my auditory chambers, where the slightest of sounds are magnified into hearing range. What others fear because they cannot hear, I hear and therefore do not fear. Not overmuch, that is. I can hear the tiny rustle of a rattlesnake's scales as it tenses to strike and is striking. I can hear the soft whirr of an owl's feathers as it drops towards what it hopes will be its prey. I can hear the infinitesimal scritch of a four-footed predator's paws in the dirt well before it has crept close enough to pounce. I do not have to sneak around hiding beneath any cover available. I can gather food out in the open. I do not have to be always looking around and up in fear because I can hear and interpret what I hear and at the right final instant unleash the springs in my splendid hindlegs and soar away. Do you read me now, man?"

"I think so," I say. "A marvelous escape technique. Never again will I regard you as merely bulgy-headed. But isn't it nerve-wracking to have such efficient hearing? All manner of sounds must be pouring in on you much of the time."

"Wrong," he says. "I simply do not hear the upper register of high frequency sounds, which have no meaning or use for me. Just about everything above the usual voice of a human male like yourself is welcome silence to me. There is quite enough to be heard down in the low frequencies—which are, of course, mere silence to you. Some are definitely pleasant like a kind of music. The rustle of grasses, for example, nodding and seeming to speak to one another in a mild breeze, can be downright exhilarating."

"I envy you your ability to hear them," I say. "But I have been wondering how to identify you. Your preference for night dark prevents me from seeing you clearly. By genus you must be a *Dipodomys*. By species do you happen to be a *spectabilis*, a bannertail?"

"Thankfully no," he says and soars straight up in the air to come down turned sideways, waving his long tail in my direction. "See. A simple, unassuming, quite adequate tuft for my steering rudder. Modest in color. Not blaring white like a bannertail's. That has always seemed to me a form of ostentatious display. If you must have a distinction for me, my species is the only one in all of this state with five toes on its hindfeet. The others get along somehow with only four. I am, therefore, an *ordii*, what you humans call an Ord's kangaroo rat. Who or what is or was the human named Ord whose tag you have attached to me I do not know or care to know. And as usual the common name you have fastened on all of my kind is all wrong. I am not a rat, precisely as my cousin the kangaroo mouse is not a mouse. We have our own family geneaology quite distinct and separate and well removed from that of the pocketless rats and mice. Call me what you will, I am still me. Happy and carefree. Glor-y-ing in my soar-y-ing.

Oops. Very bad that. I have something much better I shall use when celebrating the next special occasion. I made it up last night in my spare time. Plenty of that with so little work to do. This territory of mine is simply superb. None of the usual predators anywhere about. Seeds, nicely dried, in profusion through the sand. Obviously no one has been foraging here in a long time. I gathered a night's quota so easily I was almost ashamed of myself. Shall I give you a demonstration?"

"You confuse me," I say, "tumbling one topic after another so fast. Whatever you want to demonstrate, do it."

"My new song," he says. "Watch. Listen. This one has a drum accompaniment." Two middling jumps and he lands on a low stump, remnant of a tree cut down long ago to clear the way for the west fence line. Vaguely I can see and hear him there, body bobbing, hindfeet thumping out a tricky rhythm on the hard old wood that reminds me of a rock music beat. I begin to catch the phonetic sounds of his song:

"Er—ra—tic . . . ec-sta-tic . . .
I jump . . .
And I thump . . .
All o—ver . . . this stump!"

In one long soaring leap he is back almost where he was before, sitting up, looking at me. "And what do you think of that?"

"Wonderful," I say. "Positively splendid. So much so you will need a really special occasion to justify it. You might even have to let yourself be caught and caged again so you can escape again."

"Tricky, man, tricky," he says. "You could be thinking of volunteering to do the catching and caging. Oh no. Trust no one, said my mother."

"Not guilty," I say. "The thought had not crossed my mind. Surely you know I was joking. Let's be more serious for a moment or two. I have a question whose possible implications interest me. Perhaps you can supply an answer."

"Shoot, baby, shoot," he says. "Sock it to me."

"Damn it, rat," I say. "There you go, confusing me again. Most of the time you talk as if you held graduate degrees. And yet, now and then, you throw slang phrases at me. That seems . . ."

"Teevee, baby, teevee," says the Kangaroo Rat. "Influence of the boob tube. The idiot box. My former jailers had one of the things placed in their living room so that even when eating meals they could keep on staring at it through the kitchen door. All day long that claptrap contraption was polluting the place. The woman, first up in the morning, turned it on. The man, last to bed at night, turned it off. The daughter was glued to it when not at school or concocting wrong foods for me. No burrow I could dive into to get away from the racket. Nothing much else to do but watch it now and again and try to learn more about what makes you humans tick. But I digress. You have a question. If you will kindly phrase your interrogation in intelligible terms, I will endeavor to exercise sound judgment and respond with all seriousness. There. Is that better?"

"Much," I say. "So here goes. Our human anthropologists make much of the apparent fact that when our primate ancestors climbed down out of the trees, they learned to move about on the ground using their hindlegs only. That is, having abandoned the arboreal life, they achieved bipedal locomotion. This freed their other two limbs, now our arms-plus-hands, for (I quote an eminent authority) "the exploration and manipulation of the environment'. And that enabled them to increase their manual dexterity, which in turn was an important contributing factor in the development of our major human specialty, our brains. The very brains which have lately conceived and directed the creation of that television set you mentioned. Which, in its own turn, however asinine are some of its uses, is a marvelous achievement and a symbol of human accomplishment."

"Wordy, man, wordy," says the Kangaroo Rat. "Exposition, not a question."

"I'm getting there," I say. "Thus: the fossil record shows that the ancestors of you fellows, you kangaroo rats and mice who are not rats and mice, achieved bipedal locomotion with consequent freeing of their other limbs well before our humanoid-becoming-human ancestors achieved it. Now my question. Why, then, especially since you have had even more evolutionary time available, have you not gone ahead to develop real manual dexterity and bigger brains giving you ever greater control of the environment?"

"Let humans roar," says the Kangaroo Rat, cheerful in tone, matter-of-fact in manner. "That is less a question than an expression of human conceit. You seem to assume that your type of manual dexterity, your style of overblown brain, and your method of dealing with the environment are inevitably the goals to be sought, are the ideals in their categories. You seem to believe that other creatures, given the same opportunity, would be foolish if they failed to evolve as you have evolved."

"No, no, of course no," I say. "I do not so believe. Well, yes, perhaps I do, but not with any absolute certainty. I often have doubts that all of our human goals are good ones. At least not the only possible good ones. Obviously you fellows had somewhat the same opportunity. And obviously you evolved in a different direction. It's the whyness of that which intrigues me."

"And what is equally obvious," he says, "at least to me, is that we developed in a different direction out of instinctual wisdom and foresight. My ancestors, with forelimbs freed, did develop some manual dexterity, more than adequate for its purpose, the gathering of food. For example: I can find and pick up and pop into my pockets properly selected seeds with a speed and precision which would astonish you and which you could not possibly match. Content with that skill, my ancestors saw no sense in additional dexterity which might complicate existence without adding much if anything to the actual joy of living. They shifted attention to dexterity in soaring and in functional use of the tail. Which last is a valuable appendage you utterly lack."

"Thankfully so," I say. "To me it would be an infernal nuisance."

"Not if you could soar," he says. "But next, the other items you emphasize. Bigger brains. My ancestors were not interested in brain size, in newfangled and possibly troublesome mental gymnastics, but instead in brain adequacy for longterm survival with ever-continuing generations enjoying existence. They did a good job along that line. For example: my brain is more efficient than yours in its reception of sensory data and stimuli, in its instant interpretation of these, and in its prompt triggering of appropriate muscular action. On the survival issue I could point out that my kind has been around and doing reasonably well longer than has yours to date."

"Agreed," I say. "But I could point out that the final verdict is not yet in."

"Also agreed," he says. "So we come down to the basic difference of direction between us. You yourself have suggested the key to it. You refer to your manual dexterity and big brains as giving you ever greater control of the environment. That is precisely what my ancestors rejected as a goal, considering it a chancey choice for the long run. They opted for continued straightforward acceptance of the environment, for continuing to learn how best to live with it, for remaining a grateful and contributing part of it. Which, incidentally, is the option taken up by an overwhelming majority of all species of living creatures, including the others in your own order, the primates. On that issue you humans are vastly outvoted."

"I doubt," I say, "that the democratic notion of counting votes applies here. This is not a political but a practical matter. It is possible on such an issue that a majority, even a majority of all but one, clinging too fast to the past, could be wrong and the single solitary minority be right. It is possible that we humans have been the first to have the true wisdom and foresight to strike out in the direction of controlling the environment."

"I grant that you are the first," he says, "though I could point out that the beavers control their environment in a limited way. I refuse to admit that you are right. The test must be, as you say, the practical results. What has zealous pushing ahead in your direction done for you humans?"

"First," I say, "let me disavow any claim of complete originality for my kind. We could have picked up the basic notion from the beavers, who, after all, preceded us in the evolutionary parade. But then, foreseeing the tremendous possibilities, we have, as they have not, gone ahead to ever greater heights of accomplishment. We have devised means to live almost anywhere and everywhere, have spread throughout the world, have doubled and tripled and quadrupled our food supplies, have created innumerable mechanical and now electronic marvels, have rearranged much of the earth's surface to suit our desires, and have increased our numbers to a burgeoning four billion."

"Roar, man, roar," says the Kangaroo Rat. "Every advance you cite is based on a better-because-bigger complex, what I might call statisticitis. Numbers in themselves, beyond a minimum level, are meaningless. Quantity is not quality. Multiply four million into four billion and unless the individuals involved have improved their condition, you may merely have multiplied misery. Unless they have become happier, you may merely have multiplied unhappiness. You humans have a saying: the more the merrier. I see no evidence that the more of you there are, the merrier you become. It seems to me that as a species you have multiplied your problems almost as drastically as your numbers—and many if not most of those problems derive from your increasingly complicated gadgetry and from the sheer mass of you crowding in upon one another, fostering rivalries and hatreds, exhausting the resources of the environment you claim to be controlling. Here and there you have managed to surround quite a few of you with a clutter of material things and mechanized comforts. But the result is pathetic. Speak up, man. Tell me, baby. How many of your acquaintances are truly happy, find consistent joy in living?"

"Hold up," I say. "That's a loaded question. Before I could answer, you would have to define your terms, explain what you mean by TRULY happy, by CONSISTENT joy in living. Drop those tricky tags and I'd say some of my friends qualify. Some of the time. Naturally not all of the time. You overlook one of our special qualities which has prompted our push towards ever greater achievement and which we like to label as a divine discontent. We are never quite satisfied. We are always seeking to improve our condition."

"Rubbish and flapdoodle and poppycock," says the Kangaroo Rat. "There is nothing divine about that discontent. Actually it is nothing more than a nagging suspicion that you took a wrong direction plus an inability to see any alternative except to keep on pushing in that wrong direction. Your big brain backfires, besets you with worries and wants and jealousies and jitters that keep you forever frustrated. I used to think about that while watching the boob tube for lack of anything else to do. It ought to depress you with the picture it gives of your so-called condition. It suggests that just about every other one of you is a police officer or a private eye or a criminal and that all the rest of you suffer heart-rending personal and social problems and are in constant need of instruction in cleanliness and hygiene and the right medicines for endless ailments. It suggests that in an attempt to vent your frustrations you spend an amazing amount of time chasing about in and smashing up motor vehicles."

"Oh, come now," I say. "Everyone knows that most

teevee programs are parodies and exaggerations of reality. Their purpose is simply to entertain."

"Too often their overall effect is to disgust," he says. "But I do not base my judgment solely on them. My own experience supports what basically they say about you. I was able to observe quite a few of you at that pet store and again at the home of my temporary jailers. Each and every one was grouchy and grumbly in attitude towards existence, at odds with life in general and his or her personal condition in particular. They were all discontented all right—in a grubby greedy self-serving way. In sum: in your zeal to make maximum use of your manual dexterity and swollen brains, you humans have forgotten how to live."

He pauses, head up, intent, looking straight at me as if expecting, wanting, a prompt response. I try to comply. "Your verdict," I say, "is a harsh one, but I am compelled to accept it. At least in limited form. All too many of us are somewhat as you say. But there are some of us and hopefully . . ."

"Hang in there, baby," he says. "Stand up on those hindlegs that freed your hands and defend your kind. Don't slide around with partial agreements and limited exceptions and such. Pride in one's self and one's species should be an integral part of existence. Use that big brain and argue me down."

"I would that I could," I say. "Somehow I cannot. Perhaps because of that nagging suspicion of wrong goals you cited plus an inescapable feeling of guilt which it fosters."

"And that," he says, still cheerful and matter-of-fact as always, "may just be another boggle begot by your overblown brain. All the directions which the various creatures have taken may be good ones, each in its own way. As you noted a while ago, the verdict is not yet in. And why, after all, does there have to be a verdict? That, too, can be only a brain boggle."

"A comforting thought," I say. "Bolstered by it I ask you what are the practical results of the direction you fellows have taken?"

"Nothing spectacular," says the Kangaroo Rat. "No grandiose projects. No overrunning of the earth. No attempts to rearrange the natural world. Simply longterm survival for my kind and a zest in living which makes that survival worth while. It seems obvious to me that I find existence more rewarding than do you. I am not pestered by regrets about the past and worries about the future and desires that are beyond fulfillment. I find satisfaction in the acceptance of my natural condition and the wresting of a living from a natural environment. I live fully in each wide-awake moment of my life. I take each new night as a wondrous gift to be enjoyed, an experience to savor. I readily admit that I have no reason to roar because I am content to soar."

As if to prove that last he leaps high, seeming to spin in the air, a blurred shape in the darkness, and drops to disappear into the even darker shadow of a weed patch. His voice comes faintly to me. "If I were given to such emotions, I could feel sorry for you humans. You have forgotten how to live."

Silence. He is gone, perhaps down one of the hidden entrances to his underground home.

*   *   *

Another evening. A week or more has passed. I have been too beset by big-brained human complications of existence with their attendant worries and wants to do any ditch-bank dark-time visiting. But I am there now, waiting, watchful, wondering how he has been faring in his triangular territory.

Again, as before, drowsiness begins to take me. And again, as before, I nod awake, somehow certain that he is somewhere near. "Hello, out there," I say. "Top of the evening to you."

Silence. I sense slight movement near some clumped grasses. I try again, this time with my own little ditty patterned on his: *"Though it's getting late—I wait."*

"What for?" says the Kangaroo Rat.

There he is. He has shuffled out into the open. Shuffled is the right word. No soaring, no leaping; just a few small shuffling hops.

"For more conversation with you," I say. "What you might call a rap session. It's a lovely night for that."

"It's a lousy night," he says. "All nights are lousy. One after another and each and every one lousy."

"Wow!" I say. "That's a sharp shift from what you told me before. You certainly are low in spirit tonight."

"Low?" he says. "So low I could crawl under an earthworm's belly. You bother me. Go away."

"I will not go away," I say. An urge to try to cheer him up is rising in me. "I am going to tell you what an amazing and admirable creature I think you are. You have accepted and mastered a challenge that would defeat me utterly. So many things about you, such assets as your water conservation techniques and your superb hearing and your soaring ability, assets that are part of you and not artificial aids such as we humans have to contrive, enable you to live successfully in the difficult and deadly environment of true desert. In my opinion that puts you well ahead of any roaring tiger in any cosmic balancing of ability counts."

"No, no, of course no," he says. "That tiger has plenty of other abilities which I do not." He has perked up some and obviously, though I may not be cheering him, I have caught his interest. "As a matter of fact," he says, "that tiger can get along successfully in another kind of environment which also would defeat you utterly. Without, that is, your artificial aids."

"You mean a jungle," I say. "Well, yes. If I were talking to him, I would readily admit that he too is an amazing and admirable animal. But he is far away and you are here. Tell me. Why are you so low in spirit?"

"Basically boredom," says the Kangaroo Rat. "I might as well be in another cage. This territory of mine is too perfect. Life here is too easy, too comfortable, too secure. It has no cutting edge of risk and difficulty. There is no satisfaction in working to gather and store food when it is so plentiful. There are no neighbors of my own kind with whom I can have nerve-tingling tangles over territorial rights. There are none of our little cousins whom you call Merraim's kangaroo rats, who are persistent pilferers and who keep one alert and on guard and who sometimes have to be given good thumpings when caught raiding storerooms. And just think of it, not once in the time I have been here have I had to outjump and outwit a predator. I would not deign to consider the occasional dog who bumbles along and sniffs at one of my tunnels even a potential predator. There are no snakes, no owls, no coyotes. You humans have eliminated them all hereabouts. Life here is dull, routine, and disgustingly devoid of demand upon my abilities."

"You make it sound like that of most humans," I say. "Giving you some of the same frustrations."

"Right," he says. "And bothersome dreams. I daydream of the West Mesa of my early days where life was alive with living."

"It's still there," I say. "Not yet overrun by us wrong-directioned humans. Why don't you go there?"

"Are you out of your mind?" he says. "It's across the river. The river! Water! Huge quantities of the stuff."

"There are bridges," I say.

"Bridges? Those are things people put in their mouths. That pet store man had two and complained about them all the time."

"A different variety," I say. "Big ones. Just like roads or streets going right over the river with the water down under out of the way."

He is sitting up on his haunches, staring at me. I can almost feel the meaning of my words sinking into him. Suddenly he soars upward like a spring released and is off into a series of leaps circling here and there and everywhere. He drops to a stop closer to me than ever before. "Oh, baby," he says. "That's beautiful. What way to the nearest one of those things?"

"Slow down," I say. Second thoughts are crowding in on me. "There are only two bridges along this whole section of river and the nearest is at least five miles from here and it's another six or seven miles on the other side to the West Mesa. Much of the way through built-up areas with many streets and some major highways to get across. Considerable traffic even at night. Especially trucks. It would be . . ."

"That's your big brain at work," he says. "Worrying about mere details. All you are really saying is that it would be a difficult journey. So what? Life is to be lived even if cut short, not frittered away in futile self-defeating frustrations. As you tell it, a long way. All right. I will travel by night, hide out by day, like some of your crooks on that teevee. Just aim me at that nearest bridge and I'm already started."

"No, no, of course no," I say. "I refuse such a responsibility. It would be a damned difficult journey even for big me if I had to make it on foot." Suddenly I sit up straighter, proud of my big brain and its ability to solve problems. "You just come along," I say, "and pop into my car and I can drive you there in about half an hour."

"Your car?" he says. "Oh, no. Another kind of cage. Oh, no. Trust no one, said my mother. I'll do it on my own if it kills me."

"You're a stubborn little fool," I say, still proud of my big brain solving this too. "Look. I have a little truck. Pick-up variety. Back wide open. You ride there and any time you think I'm trying to trick you, you can simply soar out."

He stares at me again, only a few seconds this time, and is off into another series of leaps, adding mid-air somersaults, and I catch snatches of a new impromptu ditty: "*A truck! A truck! The man has a truck—what luck!* He drops down in front of me. "lead on," he says. "And thank you, sir, in advance."

"And thank you too," I say, leading the way away. "You have helped me to some pride in myself and my species. Human contrivances are not all bad. Some have really useful uses."

He is zooming with zest of living as he leaps along beside me, close but not too close. "It was another of your contrivances" he is saying, "that put me in my predicament in the first place. But that's quibbling. At a time like this I will not look a gift machine in the mouth. Why, that's pretty good. It would fetch a laugh on a boob tube program."

He prattles on, amazing me by the ease with which he clears the ditch while I have to cross on the plank laid over my watergate and again as he soars over our fence while I have to go through a gate and yet again as he soars expertly up and into the body of the truck. I can understand his delight in ditties. Free and happy in the open of the night world and on his way to what he wants, life fairly sings in him.

"Tigers," I am saying to myself as I step on the starter and head out the drive bound for the Corrales bridge and beyond. "Tigers are amazing and admirable animals. But this small mite of mortality, spurning ease and comfort and security, demanding difficulties and a cutting edge to existence, is a match for any tiger in all that really matters." Words, phrases, whole sentences for an appropriate farewell to him crowd through my mind.

No chance for them. As I slow to a stop on the narrow dirt road that has taken us up and out onto the West Mesa, I am startled by a thumping overhead. He has leaped up on the cab top and is thumping out his own rhythmic good-bye. Through the open side window I catch a glimpse of him arching well away to the ground. Peering out I see the small shape of him bounding, bouncing on, on deeper into the heart of his homeland. Snatches of song drift back. My ears are not sure of them but my mind is:

"Erratic . . . ecstatic . . .
I soar . . .
Forevermore."

. . . and a Puma and Jaguar

(Felis concolor / Felis onca)

G<small>R-R-R-R-UMPH</small>. Contemptible creatures."

"R-r-r-ough judgment. They are really quite interesting."

"N-n-n-onsense. But at least they are gone for another night."

Surprise makes me sit up, which in turn makes me realize I have been lying on my back on a slight grassy slope. As I look around remembrance begins to mesh in my mind. The zoo. My town's zoo. I came here in late afternoon to make some notes about some of the American members of the cat family, the felids. I sat down here in the shade of a small tree where I had a reasonably close view of the major ones in their barred and penned enclosures. I recall that the air was warm, the shade welcome, and that I felt drowsy. Obviously I must have fallen asleep.

I look around again. Color up the darkening western sky informs me that the sun has slipped below the horizon. The place is deserted. That is, deserted of people. Of course. It is past closing time. Yet surely those were voices I heard, voices strange and throaty yet intelligible in words.

"Gr-r-r-r-umph. One of them is still here."

Amazing. That can only have come from that jaguar stretched out in lazy posture in his enclosure, massive head resting on powerful paws.

"R-r-r-r-ight. He's been sleeping."

Amazing again. That can only have come from that puma sitting up on his haunches in the adjoining enclosure, his seeming smallish head which I know is superbly dentured turned in my direction.

"Gr-r-r-r-umph," says the Jaguar. He's a poor specimen."

I am still a bit befuddled. "What are you two talking about?" I say.

"You," says the Puma. "You and your kind. People. Humans."

I consider this from various angles, my mind clearing. I do not exactly appreciate the Jaguar's last remark. "Well," I say. "Everyone is entitled to opinions, provided he has sound reasons for them. A soundly reasoned opinion I have right now is that if you two feel you have a right to opinions about me and my kind, I have a right to ask questions."

"Ignore him," says the Jaguar.

"No," says the Puma. "Questions too can be interesting. One occurs to me. What kind of questions will he ask? After all, blocked by bars we cannot stop him from asking, but if we wish we can refuse to answer."

"Soundly reasoned," I say. "So I proceed. For a first question, this: how is it that you two, alien by nature and usual habitat and probably personal preference to what we humans call our culture, have a command of our language and profess to know considerable about us?"

"G-g-g-ood grief," says the Jaguar. "He's plain stupid."

"Perhaps," says the Puma. "Perhaps not. Like most of his kind he may merely have not bothered to use what mind he has."

The Puma shifts position to face directly towards me. "Here we are," he says, "my neighbor and myself, cooped in these incredibly confining quarters with nothing to do but eat without earning the food and sleep with fitful dreams of other more congenial places and pace back and forth for pitiful inadequate exercise. Every day, day after day, week after week, people parade past, all sizes and shapes and descriptions, most of them gabbling nonsense but some of them talking sense. We cannot get away from them, from their voices, not even in those silly artificial caves. Constantly they are thrust upon our awareness. They comprise a particularly noisy and talkative species. In time, having keen hearing and equally keen intelli gence, we learn their language and, being creatures of natural neatness and good taste, we pay most attention to those who speak well and occasionally actually use their minds when speaking."

"This one," says the Jaguar, "hasn't used his yet."

"Give me time," I say. "I might surprise you. So here's

another question. Already I note a difference between you two." I address myself directly to the Jaguar. "You, you spotted or rather rosetted package of brute power are a prejudiced rude inconsiderate grouchy . . ."

"Gr-r-r-r-umph," interrupts the Jaguar. "I am what I am and that is enough."

I address myself to the Puma. "While you, you tawny American version of the Old-World lion, are more polite, almost friendly, apparently somewhat open-minded with even a suggestion of being something of a philosopher who regards . . ."

"Thank you," interrupts the Puma. "I suppose you in- tend that as complimentary. But the tone of your talk is annoyingly patronizing."

"An unfortunate human habit," I say. "One I try to shake. Please overlook it. But to continue—under the fur, being felids, you two are remarkably similar. Why, then, the difference in temperament and attitude?"

"Hm-m-m-m," purrs the Puma. "Now *that* IS an in- teresting question. Unimportant, of course, except as stimulating curiosity, of which I seem always to have a plentiful supply." Suddenly he sits up straighter, seeming more alert, more alive. "Why, that's the answer right there! A good part of it anyway. Most of us felids have considerable curiosity. We pumas carry whole cargos of it. You humans have a saying: curiosity killed the cat. Wrong. Curiosity made the cat, the puma cat. Yes, yes, of course. Why didn't I think of this before? It is the key which unlocks the mind. It fits. It fits like . . ."

"Gr-r-r-roww," growls the Jaguar, raising his head and aiming what is plainly a look of disgust at me. "Silly human. See what you've done. You've pushed him into one of his spells. He's off again. He plays with silly notions like a silly house cat playing with a silly little mouse."

The Puma swings his head to glance at his neighbor. "Why not, Old Grumpy?" he says. "It keeps me from being outright bored with this bar-blocked existence. Gives you a chance to do your thing too, which is to growl and grump and disagree."

"Do you mean," I say to the Puma, "that the difference between you two is simply that you have more curiosity?"

"That," says the Puma. "And more. The whys and the results of things are always fascinating. Why, for example, do I have more curiosity and what are the results? So I chase an answer like—well, yes, like a house cat after a scurrying mouse. Here I go. The respective remote ancestors of myself and of Old Grumpy, differing somewhat in curiosity quotas even then, long ago set patterns, life styles, which have made us their descendants what we are today. Old Grumpy's ancestors decided they preferred warm even hottish and humid climates with plenty of plant growth around. Jungles, not forests. River valleys not uplands and semi-arid regions. They established what I regard as only a limited range. Fairly extensive in South America yet restricted even there and not much at all here in North America. Result: jaguars have not had any really wide experience of the world. They tend to be conservative in outlook, provincial in attitude, self-sufficient in habits."

"Gr-r-r-umph," says the Jaguar. "We are what we are and that is quite enough."

"On the other paw," continues the Puma, "my ancestors refused to restrict themselves in regard to climate and environment. They traveled and colonized all through

these Americas, limited only by the surrounding oceans
and the extreme cold of the Arctic. They explored and took
up residence from the southernmost part of South
America to far northward in Canada and everywhere
throughout that vast extent from sea level to high in the
mountains. They established the most extensive range of
any single species of mammal—oh, yes, we pumas are all
one species—surpassed only in recent times by you humans. Result: we pumas have had wide scope for our
curiosity, great and varied stimulation of it. We tend to be
liberal in outlook, cosmopolitan in attitude, ever open to
new experiences."

"C-c-c-onceited too," says the Jaguar. "But no matter.
You are what you are and that is always that."

"And I am what I am," I say. "Which is as full of curiosity as any puma. So another question—or, rather, a pair of
questions. One of you regards me and my kind as contemptible, the other as interesting. In each case I ask why,
in what ways?"

The dusk has deepened and both of them are shadowy
shapes in their enclosures. I wonder which one, if a one,
will respond.

"Hm-m-m-m-m," purrs the Puma. "Old Grumpy, you
go first. You grumble that I talk too much. You take a
turn."

"Gr-r-r-umph," says the Jaguar. "I will be brief and
blunt. The basic fact is that you humans remind me of the
ants and termites of my native jungle. You are important
only in multiplied masses. An individual human being is a
weak, spindly, trembly, inefficient creature. Without the
help of myriads of his fellows he is simply a cipher, a
nothing. An ant. A termite."

"Or a honey-bee," says the Puma.

"Yes," says the Jaguar. "A honey-bee. Just one of a multitude who is insignificant in himself and achieves significance only by being one of a swarm. But an ant is the best parallel. In my experience ants are mean and nasty and vicious just like humans. From what I overhear of the talk of visitors passing by, humans are nowadays crowding ever more into towns and cities that resemble anthills. They are becoming ever more dependent on each other and so doing are moving towards true ant societies."

He pauses. I feel he is waiting for some reaction from me. "You may be right," I say. "In part at least. But we too are what we are. Can you not accept that?"

"I might," says the Jaguar. "All of us living creatures are what evolution has made us. But in regard to humans it is their hypocrisy which I regard as particularly contemptible. I first began to understand this years ago when I was quite young and still following my mother and she was killed by a human hunter. I saw it happen from where I was hidden in thick bushes and I have thought about it often through the long years since in the light of what I have learned about humans. That killing was pure wanton viciousness. That hunter had no valid reason for it. She was no danger to him, was trying to avoid him. She was no danger to others of his kind because we jaguars have never preyed on humans. That hunter did not want her body for food. He did not need her fur to cover and protect the unwholesome nakedness of his own body because he was already equipped with clothes. He wanted only her head to keep as a trophy to bolster his shrunken and inadequate ego. But I digress. I was speaking of the hypocrisy involved, which has come clear to me from the talk of people stopping here by my cage. For example: just the other day a human said here that once he had killed a jaguar in Brazil and he proceeded to tell of it. A replica of the killing of my mother. But to the point. He claimed HE killed that jaguar. He did not. Thousands upon thousands of humans combined to kill it. Some invented and designed and built the plane that took him to Brazil. Some invented and built the jeep that took him into the jungle. Some invented and made the gun and the bullets he used. He could not even have tracked and found that jaguar by himself. He had dogs and what he called 'beaters' to find his victim and bring it to bay. Yet he claims that he did the deed. He did only one small and relatively insignificant part of it. Yet he boasts that he did it. He was an ant made formidable only by the help of multitudes of ants. In his talk and even in his thoughts he is a contemptible hypocrite."

"R-r-r-ight," says the Puma. "Human minds work that way. Each individual thinks he does this or does that—yet virtually everything he does would be impossible for him without the help of thousands of others. Old Grumpy, I begin to like your ant metaphor."

It is nearly dark now and all I can make out clearly of those two is the faint glow of their eyes which I know are reflecting with small natural mirrors at the back of each eye the light of a street lamp more than one hundred yards away. Both are looking at me in what I sense are accusing stares. Knowledge that with their much more capable eyesight they can see me better than I can see them makes me somewhat nervous. Inevitably I feel called upon to defend my own kind.

"Hypocrisy aside," I say. "What you are really talking about is cooperation among us humans. By cooperating with each other we achieve infinitely more than any one of us could alone. The facts . . ."

"Exactly the same can be said of the ants," says the Puma.

"Forget your ants," I say. "The analogy is as full of holes as any anthill. As I was saying, the facts prove that our way of cooperating is superior to your felid way of what one of you has referred to as self-sufficiency. The simple fact that you two are penned here while I am free to go where I please is itself proof of our superiority."

"Gr-r-r-r-umph," growls the Jaguar. "Superiority, yes. But superiority in what? And by what means? You humans pride yourselves on your evolutionary specialty, your swollen brains. The true value of any specialty lies in the uses to which it is put. To what uses do you put yours? Primarily and basically to viciousness, to selfishness, to arrogant disregard for other forms of life. One of your own analogies is apt. You behave in this world which is the homeland of all creatures like a bull in a china shop, wreaking havoc, smashing, destroying. You lack any saving humility. Consider this: if others, we felids for example, who preceded you in development, had let ourselves develop similar motives, you would not be here today, your kind would have been rendered extinct in the very infancy of its development. Our specialty is physical power plus armament, that is, strength and agility plus scimitar claws and steel-trap jaws. You humans then as now were individually what I said before, weak spindly trembly things. You had not yet multiplied into masses and invented diabolical devices. Had we been afflicted with a persistent viciousness like yours, we could have hunted you down and erased you from the face of the earth—as you have done and are doing to so many species of fellow creatures."

"Fine words," I say, trying without much success to sound sarcastic. "Why didn't you? What stopped you?"

"Innate decency," says the Jaguar. "Something left out of the makeup of your species as a whole. Though we were and are efficient hunters and killers, we have always, except in very rare and abnormal instances, hunted and killed for food alone and never for more food than we need and can use. Always we have respected the natural predator-prey relationship, keeping our numbers consistent with the ecological balance of our habitats, and as a result the other forms of life on which we prey have lived on in their own adequate numbers. Back when you were just emerging from the humanoid into the human stage some of us occasionally preyed on you. But we soon, again except in rare and abnormal instances, stopped that."

"Aha," I say. "Was it that you learned to be afraid of us?"

"Afraid?" says the Jaguar. "The word has no meaning for us felids except as a human concept. Fear, as you humans conceive it and know it, is alien to us. Caution and a proper attention to survival are something else. No, we ceased to consider you proper prey because, by the time you had become completely human, you had acquired a foul smell and a foul taste. No respectable carnivore would willingly and by choice dine on you when other and finer prey was available. Which, incidentally, has been one of your own survival assets you never seem to recognize as such."

"R-r-r-ight," says the Puma. "But you humans at least recognize that your smell is bad. You use all manner of artificial scents to try to hide it even from each other."

"Nothing can hide it," says the Jaguar. "To a nose like mine it always comes through. I have never tasted human meat. I have no desire ever to do so. One whiff and I know it would definitely be distasteful. I would have to be on the verge of starving before I would try it—and even then I'm sure I would gag getting it down."

"You are not exactly tasteful yourself," I say. A weak rejoinder but no other occurs to me. "A friend of mine who used to do a lot of hunting told me he once tried jaguar steak. He said it was very tough and tasted awful.

"No doubt it did," says the Jaguar. "He should have known better. My kind is not the rightful prey of your kind—except from your depraved point of view as an outlet for your viciousness. But enough is enough. I have talked too much."

He lowers that massive head onto his powerful paws. That is, I surmise he does because through the darkness now between us I see his eyes with their twin shines sink down. Then they blink out. He has closed them.

"Hm-m-m-m," purrs the Puma. "A good talking. I'll say this for you. You stirred Old Grumpy into saying more than I usually can."

"He has answered my question," I say. "But with additions unnecessary and unpleasant. He certainly is what he is—which is precisely what I said he is. Now it is your turn. Why do you find us humans interesting? I hope your answer is softer, less harsh."

"A foolish hope," says the Puma. "You have me wrong. I agree absolutely with everything he has said tonight. But I am not as self-sufficient, as strong-minded as he is. I cannot face facts as firmly, let my thoughts stop where his stop, simply and gallantly confronting reality. If I did, I would brood on injustice and go mad. So, to retain my sanity, I push on seeking the whys and the results of things and the possibilities of the future. I find you humans interesting because there is so much to be learned about you—and because the more I do learn the more it seems to me that you are one of evolution's major mistakes. No. I can think of no other even remotely comparable. You are THE major mistake."

"Ouch!" I say. "That hits where it hurts. Worse than mere name-calling. How do you reach such a deadly verdict?"

"From many angles," says the Puma. "I could point out that for the first time in all of time on this spinning planet one single species, your species, is dominant throughout the whole of the habitable world. I could point out that this species is incredibly destructive, incredibly wasteful, despoiling the lands, polluting the seas and the air, spreading ruin ever more widely for ever more other forms of life, choking away ever more of the great variety and diversity nature has striven through long ages to achieve. Those are merely facts, realities, to be confronted as Old Grumpy confronts them. But how did it happen? What went wrong? What mistake was made?"

"I can recognize rhetorical questions when I hear them," I say. "Obviously you have what you think is an answer. Go ahead. Give it."

"Of course," says the Puma. "The basic question: what happened? The answer: you happened. You humans happened. Too quickly. You developed your specialty, brainpower, much too fast, actually in what can be called a mere tick or two of the evolutionary clock. Moreover, that development was not only too fast; it was also both too good and too poor."

"Ouch again!" I say. "You are going too fast. Slow down

and do some explaining before you lose me."

"Certainly," says the Puma. "First, what I mean by 'too fast.' In the normal course of evolution the development of any specialty which will have a significant impact on the environment of its possessors, in particular on their fellow creatures, has taken a long time, has been a relatively gradual process. As a result those fellow creatures have had the opportunity to make adaptations of their own, to develop new, or improve their already-existent, specialties sufficiently to withstand the impact and maintain a reasonable ecological balance. Your own students of evolution have pointed out that it is fairly certain that extinctions of species in the long past have been caused by changes in environment, in climates and habits, never by the predation of fellow creatures. Let me offer an example of my meaning: our felid specialty, which Old Grumpy mentioncd a while ago, was not developed in a hurry. Our prey, those who could suffer from its impact, had time along with us to develop and improve their defenses, their own assets for survival. The balance was maintained. Both of us, predators and prey, continued to do quite well. But with all too sudden swiftness you humans have developed your specialty. Its destructive impact is now all too apparent almost everywhere around the world."

"Gr-r-r-umph," comes from the Jaguar's enclosure. "Viciousness. Selfishness. Arrogance."

I ignore him. "You have a point there," I say to the Puma's twin eye-shines. "Our anthropologists generally agree that we developed our special capabilities at an unusually rapid rate. Let that cover the 'too fast.' How about the 'too good'?"

"Your specialty," says the Puma, "coupled with your

manual dexterity is too good in that it is too efficient, and there is too much mere cleverness involved. This enables you to avoid the difficult task of making improvements in yourselves—instead you substitute improvements in your artifacts, the things you make to compensate for your personal deficiencies. Consider weapons. Lacking personal armament, you devise substitutes. Perhaps the idea itself is sound—if applied with a decent concern for natural balances. But what do you do? In swift succession you move from the thrown rock and the swung club to the javelin and the spear, then almost immediately on to the bow and arrow. In another quick leap you achieve gunpowder and the gun and in rapid succession ever more powerful ones plus such things as the telescopic sight. What happens when some of you propose to make hunting more of a sporting proposition by returning to use of the bow and arrow? At once you get busy devising ever better bows and ever more deadly arrows. Efficiency, prompted by your personal pathetic deficiencies, is an obsession with you. Always you seek the extra advantage. That is why your impact has been so destructive. The obsession with efficiency backed by your cleverness in implementing it runs through virtually every human activity—even to that of humans destroying humans."

"Gr-r-r-umph. Like ants. Ant colonies fighting one another."

I ignore this too. "Strange," I say to the Puma, "that you should downgrade efficiency. You felids are supposed to be very efficient in your way, probably the most efficient of hunters, for instance, next to us humans. Aren't you proud of your efficiency?"

"No," says the Puma. "Satisfied with it, yes. Proud of it,

no. Pride has no place in such matters. Adequacy does. No doubt, should we put our minds and muscles to it, we could tally impressive totals of prey carcasses—as human hunters often do. Personally, what I am proud of is that we do not, that we refuse to push our efficiency past simple adequacy. In effect we merely impose a limited tax in lives on our prey species and one which over the generations primarily culls out the weak and maladjusted of those species and helps keep their breeding stock healthy and well adapted for continued survival. Moreover, we keep that tax levy within reasonable limits by keeping our own numbers within reasonable limits. We do this by deliberate use of privacy in hunting territories and a relatively slow reproductive rate. It is a plain fact that under natural conditions—which is to say, when no humans are around to push in and interfere—our populations and the populations of our prey species remain remarkably constant through the years."

"Gr-r-r-umph. There were always deer and peccaries aplenty until human efficiency went to work on them."

I manage to ignore this too. "I follow you," I say to the Puma. "Which does not mean I agree with everything you say. You've covered 'too fast' and 'too good.' Now comes 'too poor'."

"R-r-r-ight," says the Puma. "Your human specialty is too poor in that it is lopsided. Your brain-power is unbalanced. It has motor power and no brakes. It has remarkable cleverness in devising ways and means of accomplishing whatever you think you want to do, but it is weak towards the vanishing point in foresight, in seeing forward and recognizing probable consequences. To be blunt: you make constant mistakes, proving my assertion that you yourselves are a mistake."

"Fine words," I say. "But vague. Generalities only. Give me examples. What kind of mistakes?"

"For one," says the Puma, "when you have started something, you rarely know when to stop. Consider weapons again. As noted before, you need artificial ones to compensate for your deficiencies. But once started making them, you keep right on, driven by that efficiency obsession, until you have devised the ultimate weapons, atomic weapons, which can destroy us all, yourselves included. You achieve an absolute absurdity: weapons so effective that they cannot be used. More correct: should not be used. Yet the chances are strong that they will be used. Unbalanced brain-power at work. Never yet have you devised a weapon which sooner or later has not been used."

"But we have," I say. "There are other weapons in our arsenals we have not used. Powerful new poison gases, toxic substances to be put in water supplies, diseases to be deliberately spread, and many others. I am afraid, however, that they simply support your point that we have carried weaponry to its ultimate absurdity."

"Gr-r-r-r-umph. Not absurdity. Obscenity."

"Of course," says the Puma. "But I proceed to another kind of mistake, result of your failure to foresee consequences. Consider pesticides. To protect your food crops from the ravages of insects you formulate poisonous substances designed to kill them. Which do kill them. Some of them. Even quite a large number of them. In the short-range view you are successful. But you fail to foresee that those, even though few, who do not die obviously have some form of immunity to your poisons and can soon build up big populations again most of whom will have similar immunity. Because of the multiplicity of insect progeny and the swift succession of their generations, that does not take long. You fail to see that you are creating an artificial selection process replacing the natural. You are forced to devise ever different and stronger poisons—and at the same time you are helping the insects to develop ever greater immunity and destructive power. You are actually aiding them in what may be their own drive to achieve dominance in the world. The same can be said of your use of those relatively new medicines known as antibiotics. By the same process you are aiding harmful bacteria to develop ever greater immunity and virulence. In pursuit of presumed present advantages, you disregard future disadvantages. Unbalanced brain power at work."

"Gr-r-r-umph. Nothing but stupidity. Stupidity."

"The Puma ignores this as I do. He is in full verbal stride. "I am continually astounded," he says, "at the number of human activities which fit that pattern. But I move on, will be content with one more example of a kind of mistake, that of going only halfway in what could be a good project and refusing to accept the other half. Consider your notion that human life is sacred and must be protected and saved in any way possible. I understand the notion as a natural one, but I condemn the way in which you apply it. You push it towards the extreme—and virtually ignore the responsibility it entails. By striving to eliminate all hazards, by reducing infant mortality and by saving and prolonging lives, you drive ahead straight into overpopulation of your species. You ignore, or at best make only feeble efforts to meet, the obligation involved, that of devising equally efficient methods of population control.

You are the one species of mammal in this Age of Mammals which refuses to accept natural limitations on population overgrowth. To be blunt again: in this respect you are a cancerous growth let loose in the world's biosphere."

"Enough," I say. "I have heard more than enough in that vein."

"No," says the Puma. "You started this discussion. You asked for it. So I insist upon summarizing my position. Behind all the mistakes I have been citing which make you humans a mistake is the attitude with which you insist upon confronting the mysterious miracle of life on this earth. You are in constant rebellion against the facts of existence. You refuse to accept that you too are part of the natural order and that this imposes obligations for the good of us all, including yourselves. You refuse to fit into the over-all scheme of things and instead strive blindly to make it fit you. In a strange sort of blindness you consider yourselves something apart and above the inescapable rules governing all living creatures. And thus you push inevitably towards ultimate self-destruction—which, alas, may include most or all of the rest of us."

"Gr-r-r-umph. Too fancy. Make it simple. Viciousness and selfishness and arrogance."

That Jaguar is impossible. He does not reason, simply asserts. The Puma is opinionated, yes, but he does seem to be somewhat open to argument. Somehow I feel that he would like me to try, to be able, to refute him. I itch to make the attempt. But I recall there remains one item I want him to cover. "You used another phrase which requires explaining," I say. "You mentioned 'the possibilities of the future.' Possibilities. Plural. Perhaps, then, catastrophe is not the only possibility you think possible."

"R-r-r-ight," says the Puma. "As Old Grumpy suggested, I am like a house cat scurrying after mice and hoping to catch the right one. Perhaps I should have more faith in whatever power, call it a god or a prime mover or a providence or whatever you will, lies behind the evolutionary process. Perhaps I should have more faith in the evolutionary process itself. Perhaps it has its own balancing mechanism which in the long swing of time corrects its own mistakes—as perhaps has happened on occasions in the past. Among us felids, for example, there were some who went in for excessive specialization in weaponry. I refer to the sabertooths. Nowadays we more moderate felids are still here, but the sabertooths have vanished. Or again, think of the reptiles, who once dominated active life on earth. Some of them went in for exaggerations in size, and others in weaponry, became what I believe can be called mistakes. What happened? Reptiles are still with us, but those exaggerations are extinct. Excessive specialization finally takes its toll."

"Are you implying," I say, "that we humans have gone in for an excessive specialization, our brain-power, and that this will take its toll, in effect ultimately eliminate us?"

"That is one possibility," says the Puma. "You may represent an exaggeration of the mammalian mode of life which evolution's balancing mechanism will be forced to eliminate. But that possibility is tainted with cosmic injustice because the probable process, that of your destructive capabilities turning back upon you, might well be either atomic blastings with their aftermath of radiation or a slow strangulation as your other works render most of the world uninhabitable. In either case the process would have a terrible and unjust impact upon all the rest of us. I prefer to ponder another possibility."

"I hope," I say, "that it contains some optimism."

"It does," says the Puma. "Consider the fact that you humans are such a relatively recent addition to the mammalian roster. While it is true that in evolutionary terms no life form can be said to be finished unless or until it becomes extinct, in a relative sense perhaps you humans can be said to be unfinished, not really much more than started, still in a sort of experimental stage. Perhaps further evolution will not eliminate you but instead will continue to develop you in ways that will eliminate the necessity of eliminating you."

"Gr-r-r-r-umph. Fine words. False hope."

It is easier this time to ignore that Jaguar. "Thank you," I say to the Puma, "for that second possibility. And I want to point out something that has been in my mind ever since you started your lecture. Blanket denunciations do not fit us humans. We are a remarkably various species. And some of us recognize much more than you give us credit for. Just about everything you have said has been said in one form or another by some of us."

"Of course," says the Puma. "How do you imagine I have obtained data for my pondering except by listening to those of you who come by here discussing such matters. I doubt, however, that those particular humans can be regarded as indications that the evolutionary corrective process I have just mentioned has begun. They are very few among very many others—and I notice that, unlike most of those others, they rarely have children with them. They are poor reproducers and probably add little if anything significant to your human gene pool. Moreover, I also note that many of your human efforts are aimed at alleviating or preventing the very means of natural selection by which evolution operates. . . . But now I want to thank you in turn. I feel better, having had the opportunity to speak my mind to one of your kind. You do seem to be rather a decent specimen after all. Eh, Old Grumpy, do you agree?"

"Gr-r-r-umph. He's passable. Passable. But still a mistake."

As he says this the Jaguar raises his head and his twin eye-shines show plainly. He is looking at or past me. He voices a curious small grunting sound which I cannot interpret and the Puma replies in the same peculiar manner. I sense a comradely rapport between these two.

"Enough of such serious matters," says the Puma. "Something more entertaining is in order. It occurs to me that you humans often argue whether or not we pumas scream. Like a woman or child in mortal agony is, I believe, the way some of you describe it. Well, yes, we do emit some rather high-pitched sounds, though we usually reserve them to accompany the desires and ecstasies of mating. Shall I provide an example?"

"No, no, no. There's no . . ." I start to say In vain. The Puma is raising his head higher and from him comes a wonderfully high-pitched, ear-piercing wailing sound that has a nerve-tingling wildness in it. And from the Jaguar's enclosure, as if to provide background, comes a deep-throated coughing roar that sends chills chasing themselves up and down my spine.

These sounds cease, leaving a sudden stillness. And in that stillness I hear or at least sense new sounds like shoes treading on grass behind me. I whirl around—and a beam of bright light strikes me full in the face, virtually blinding me.

"Whatinell d'you think you're doin' here?" says an all-too-human voice.

The light lowers, playing on my middle region and hanging hands. Vaguely I can make him out now, a solid-built human-shaped figure holding a flashlight in one hand and a sample of human weaponry in the other. A night watchman. A security guard.

"One of them nasties," he says. "Stirrin' up the animals."

I try to explain what I have been doing. Sheer foolishness. I am a mistake making a mistake, not using my supposed specialty, my brain-power. Obviously he regards me as some kind of a possibly dangerous lunatic. He orders me to shut up, to turn around, to put my hands behing my back. I feel and hear handcuffs click around my wrists.

"Come along," he says. "It's a night in jail for you—and you can try that kind of crazy talk on a judge in the mornin'."

As he leads me away, more sounds come from those two barred enclosures, sounds which I am sure are to him simply grumps and growls confirming his belief that I have been stirring up the animals. Alas, to me they are all too understandable.

"Gr-r-r-umph. Didn't he say he was superior because he could go where he pleased?"

"R-r-r-ight. But I don't think he pleases to go to spend a night in jail—and likely pay a fine in the morning."

OTHER BOOKS BY JACK SCHAEFER

FICTION

SHANE (novel)
FIRST BLOOD (novel)
THE BIG RAIN (stories)
THE CANYON (novel)
THE PIONEERS (stories)
COMPANY OF COWARDS (novel)
THE KEAN LAND & OTHER STORIES
OLD RAMON (juvenile)
MONTY WALSH (novel)
STUBBY PRINGLES' CHRISTMAS (juvenile)
MAVERICKS (novel)

NONFICTION

THE GREAT ENDURANCE HORSE RACE (history)
HEROES WITHOUT GLORY (biography)
THIS NEW MEXICO (history)
AMERICAN BESTIARY (zoology)
CONVERSATIONS WITH A POCKET GOPHER (revelations)